**SMALL
MEDIUM**

**LARGE
IMPACT**

SMALL MEDIUM
LARGE IMPACT

*The Miracle of
World Mission Radio*

Dean Nelson

Nazarene Publishing House
Kansas City, Missouri

10   9   8   7   6   5   4   3   2   1

To my wife, Marcia, who helped teach me
how to communicate
To Paul Miller, who got me started as a writer
To Dean Spencer, who taught me a lot about life
and whom I miss deeply

Dean Nelson codirects the journalism program at Point Loma Nazarene College in San Diego, Calif. He holds an M.A. in journalism from the University of Missouri-Columbia and a Ph.D. in journalism and mass communication from Ohio University. He writes for several newspapers and magazines throughout the country, including the *New York Times* and the *Boston Globe*.

Dean, his wife, Marcia, and two children, Blake and Vanessa, reside in San Diego.

Contents

Introduction

Elario Zugina is an intense, educated man who lives in San Ramon, Costa Rica, with his wife and three children. He is intense about his work, his family, and his desire to know God. His intensity caught the eye of the Catholic church he attended, and the church officials selected him as one of the lay leaders for a neighborhood group to discuss theology and set membership guidelines.

"This activity gave me the opportunity to study the basics of the Bible, without the permission of the priest," he said. "It began in me a period of serious searching."

During the next two years of searching, he also attended Bible studies with a local Charismatic group, and he allowed the Jehovah's Witnesses to conduct meetings in his home.

"But while I was involved in these groups and studying my Bible, I realized that some of what they were telling me wasn't what the Bible was telling me, so I ended my association with all of them," he said. His work transferred him to the Atlantic coast of Costa Rica, where he listened to many religious broadcasts on the radio.

"Most of the programs were excellent, but they were tied solely to the person giving the sermon," he said. "I wondered to myself, 'Why isn't there a church somewhere that believes like these programs or believes what the Bible teaches?'"

There was good news for Zugina. He heard a program called "La Hora Nazarena" (The Nazarene Hour) and heard the following at the end of the broadcast: "Brought to you by your friends at the Church of the Nazarene."

"When I heard that statement, I knew I had to find out more about that church," he said. He returned to San Ramon and looked in the phone book. The closest Nazarene church he could find was in San Jose, about a two-hour drive, but the church sent two people to his home to talk with him. After a few visits they helped Zugina begin his personal walk with Jesus Christ. There are now 11 Bible studies in San Ramon as a result.

Zugina is a changed man. So is his family, and so is San Ramon. He heard the gospel, acted on what he heard, and became tied to a church. And his world will never be the same. Amid all of his experiences and searching, the key was the radio program.

There are billions of other Elario Zuginas in the world —some living in countries where radio is the dominant medium for information and entertainment and some where it is not. But even in countries where the popularity of radio has been surpassed by television, radios are still on. Millions are still listening. In countries where video is still decades away and where illiteracy makes printed materials difficult to use, radio is the only choice.

The good news for Elario Zugina is the same good news the rest of the world can hear: There is a God who loves us and a Son who saves us. That message is heard around the world, and, in most cases, listeners can be brought into a fellowship of believers whose lives have been changed by that message.

This book tells the story of how the Church of the Nazarene committed itself to using radio as a means to proclaim the message, and how the medium is used as a ministry tool to change people's lives. It is a look back to the beginning, nearly 50 years ago for the English-speaking broadcasts, and 40 years for the Spanish-speaking broadcasts. It is also a look to the future. Most of all, though, it is a book about people who choose to proclaim the message in this far-reaching way, and those who have come to believe in Jesus Christ through the airwaves.

1

An End to the Famine

In 1989, in an area that was then known as the Soviet Union, resistance to Communist rule boiled over. Soviet leader Mikhail Gorbachev had been gingerly trying to connect his nation with the rest of the world through a more open attitude toward the West and through a more open attitude toward members of the Soviet Union. Simultaneously, he was trying to allow economic changes to take place that would put less emphasis on government controls. Glasnost, as the new openness was called, and Perestroika, the effort to reform the economy, made Gorbachev a popular man outside of the Soviet Union. In Europe, the United States, and China, for instance, parades honored him when he came to visit, and millions of citizens lined the streets shouting "Gorby! Gorby! Gorby!" *Time* magazine had already declared him its Man of the Year.

But the nation was quickly crumbling from within. Provinces demanded their independence from the union of regions that had been forced together after World War II. Some revolted in an effort to end the Soviet domination that had been forced on them for more than 40 years. Communism was seen not as the answer but as the problem. The resentment over the ruthless practices of Lenin and Stalin was growing rapidly, and people were even encouraged to question those tyrannies. The government called home its troops from Afghanistan, further eroding the perception of the nation's strength.

To the 285 million people within its seemingly endless boundaries, it was clear that major changes were occurring. The Soviet Union of 1989 was different from the Soviet Union of 1979, 1969, 1959, and 1949. The changes were occurring faster than at any point since Peter the Great opened Russian doors to the West nearly 300 years before. In a nation known for its religious persecutions, candidates for public office were being asked during televised debates whether they believed in God.

One additional piece of evidence regarding the changes could be heard at Christmastime that year. A 30-minute program telling the Christmas story, sponsored by the Church of the Nazarene, was broadcast into the U.S.S.R. The program had Russian folk singers playing Christmas music, giving sermonettes, and discussing the theme of how much God must have loved us to have sent His Son in the form of a baby to save us from our sins. Similar broadcasts were aired in Bulgarian, Armenian, Turkish, and other languages. This was a true sign of Glasnost!

One week later, another Nazarene-sponsored program was broadcast for New Year's Day. At the end of both programs, a post office box number in Moscow was given, and listeners were encouraged to write to the program. After only two broadcasts, the post office box received more than 125 responses. Listeners requested Bibles, more information on Christ, and asked for counseling.

"It is difficult for people to believe that God exists after 70 years of being told that He doesn't," wrote one listener. "They recently published the Gospel of Matthew in 'The World of Books,' a Soviet magazine. I am telling people to go to the library and read it. I believe there will come a day when we can hear the gospel not only on the radio, but also on television!"

Another listener expressed amazement that God could be discussed publicly.

"Who could have imagined that we would be able to openly talk about God without being put in prison," she wrote. "We can freely distribute Bibles, and people accept them without embarrassment."

Some letters were more reserved in their judgments of the programs, but they showed an interest nonetheless.

"I want to make one thing very clear," wrote one man. "I am an atheist; in other words, a person who doesn't believe in the existence of God. You are offering to send a Bible without any conditions. I don't think the Bible will cause me to become a church member, but it would be interesting to read it."

Christian activity in the Soviet Union had been expanding for years, although it was an underground movement. Who would ever have dreamed that the gospel would be so accessible when, 35 years ago, Bibles were secretly made available through means like the following scene:

> That afternoon at one o'clock we pulled up in front of the GUM store. A man emerged from a car parked a hundred yards away and strolled by, looking at us cautiously through the window. Then he strolled back again.
>
> "Brother Andrew?"
>
> "You're Markov," I said. "Greetings in the Name of the Lord."
>
> "We're going to do something very bold," said Markov, talking rapidly. "We're going to exchange the Bibles within two minutes of Red Square. No one will ever suspect us in such a location. It's a stroke of genius."
>
> Clearly, this brother was more of a genius than I. I didn't like the sound of it. He led us to a street that was, sure enough, less than two minutes from Red Square. There was a large blind wall running along one side of the street, but houses lined the other. At any window could be a pair of curious eyes.
>
> "You'd better pray," I said to Hans as I parked behind Markov's car.
>
> Hans did pray aloud, as I got out the Bibles and stowed them an armload at a time into cartons and sacks. Markov opened the rear door to his car, and we made the transfer

right out in the open, trip after trip on the busy sidewalk. When we were finished, Markov allowed himself time only for a quick handshake apiece before he was back in his car starting the engine.[1]

Had the smugglers been caught, they would have faced the same penalty as those caught smuggling pornography—Bibles and pornography were considered similar material by the government.

But the underground Christians persevered and made desperate requests to Christian organizations for programs to be broadcast into their country. In 1984, Trans World Radio invited representatives from the Church of the Nazarene to participate in developing evangelistic programs for the Soviet Union. Trans World Radio is an international, interdenominational Christian organization that produces and broadcasts Christian programs around the world, through the cooperation of numerous evangelical organizations. The Church of the Nazarene had worked with Trans World for many years throughout the world, and Trans World was seeing the possibility of a unique opportunity for radio ministry in the U.S.S.R.

The Christians in the Soviet Union said underground broadcasts weren't meeting needs, and the political climate was appearing to allow bolder efforts. They wanted help developing meaningful programs in better facilities than the basements they had been using. They wanted help training people in the use of radio as a means for ministry.

"We believe in responding to opportunities and taking the initiative, which in this case was in tune with what was happening in the Soviet Union," said Ray Hendrix, director of international publications for the Church of the Nazarene. He said there were approximately 50,000 "radio congregations" in the Soviet Union.

"These are congregations that have existed with their only instruction and inspiration coming from the radio," he said. "People were searching for something, and they were really disenchanted with their own political and religious systems in areas of the world where freedom of religion did not exist.

"Wherever they hear messages that promise free forgiveness of sin, they start to realize that this is a unique aspect of a religion that they had never heard of before. This really captivates their attention, and they want to listen."

The meetings with Trans World Radio evolved into plans for developing programs, facilities, and training. Coupled with the rapid political changes of the late 1980s, the programs were ready for the holidays at the end of 1989.

Through much of 1990 another radio program called "The Beacon of Hope" was broadcast monthly, with young people as the target audience. The themes included discussion of salvation, the work of the Holy Spirit, sin, compassion, and freedom in Christ.

By October the program was broadcast weekly. The segments were recorded in Russia by Russian Christians, in facilities built and financed by the Church of the Nazarene through offerings and Work and Witness teams. It was then sent over the airwaves by powerful Trans World Radio transmitters in Monte Carlo, Cyprus, and Guam.

The hunger for the message offered in "The Beacon of Hope" was seen that year when a small advertisement was placed in the classified section of the Russian newspaper *Isvestia* (another sign of Glasnost!) that said, "If you feel you have been lied to and don't know what truth is, cheer up. There is truth. Listen to 'The Beacon of Hope.' For more information and a free copy of the Gospel of John, write to this address." More than 47,000 people responded to that ad.

One other Russian noted a different kind of item in another publication. While a student at the European Nazarene Bible College in Switzerland, Nikolaj Sawatzky was reading the news summary page of *World Mission* magazine. He saw a news report about the Nazarene-sponsored broadcasts in Russia.

"That article interested me greatly, so I told the Department of World Mission that I would like to help," he said. Sawatzky is now involved in following up on letters written to the program, in church planting, and in helping develop radio programs. The letters are providing a base of contacts for development of churches, and already there are several laymen conducting Bible studies with the help of the broadcasts.

"The Russian government is open to our type of programs, to say the least," Sawatzky said. "Even the state-owned radio stations are requesting programs. People are amazed that these broadcasts are being done, but the positive nature and the number of responses has been very big." Most of those responding want to know more about the messages, and ask for Bibles or other reading materials.

One listener said the change in his life was almost immediate.

"In a very short time your radio programs have completely changed my worldview," he wrote. "I hadn't heard anything like it before. Now I want to read God's Book."

How hard was it to get a copy of the Bible?

"It is easier for us to get to the moon than to get a Bible," a man wrote.

Another listener hoped that there were answers to the questions she raised.

"I am 39 years old and I am living in complete darkness," she wrote. "I want to find the truth, to understand the meaning of life. I have three questions: Where did I come from? Where am I going? and Where will I be after I die? I am far from God, but inside of me there is this unknown voice urging me to seek the Creator. Your programs have caused me to think about the meaning of life on earth. I am at the crossroads."

The programs helped another man find Christ.

"I was saved through the radio programs and this year I was baptized in the Dnepr River," he wrote.

The joy for some listeners is in part how easily accessible the programs are now.

"God is doing great things in our country," wrote one listener. "Your radio programs are God's living Word, His bread, and we don't have to stand in line for it! We can sit at home and receive food ready to eat!"

Sawatzky has additionally been trained in various aspects of broadcasting.

"We have a great need right now for more people who can be trained in this area so we can record, produce, broadcast, and follow up on our own programs," Sawatzky said. "The programs are more effective when they are produced by other Russians who are experiencing the life there. It is difficult to find the people trained for this, though."

As more people are trained, broadcasts can be diversified to speak to family and youth issues and children's programs, and then into some of the 150 languages spoken in the enormous region. A communications center will be built in Moscow by Work and Witness teams, and the hope is that enough people can be trained to develop programs from within the country.

"Our biggest prayer request is for finding people to serve in this field," Sawatzky said.

Programs that are locally produced are more likely to be aired on local stations, said Ray Hendrix, and the key to this kind of production is finding and equipping people in Russia to carry it out. As political changes continue to occur in the former Soviet region, there is a feeling that now is the time to be acting on the opportunities that have become available. Some groups are doing this, and Hendrix said the church's hope is that it can find the people and the resources to capitalize on the spirit of openness.

"My sense of urgency is not that the doors are going to close soon," Hendrix said, "but that cults and other groups are moving in faster and better than we are. Islam and New Age, McDonald's and IBM all have strategies. We have one, too, but we are hampered by a lack of resources and personnel."

Still, courage and direction can be drawn from letters like this one.

"I am a member of an unregistered church. For over 50 years we hid ourselves and fought for survival. We suffered in the Siberian forests, but we continued to preach the gospel; we were not silent. But it is hard for us to readjust; we are accustomed to being on the defensive, and now we need to go on the offensive, attack, conquer the cities. It is difficult to feed the multitudes with Living Bread after so many years of famine."

As it has in so many regions around the world, the Church of the Nazarene, sensing God's direction through prayer, circumstance, and dedicated believers, is helping bring an end to the famine.

Then, leaning forward, he asked another question. "Tell me, my friend, why did you really come to Russia?"

On the tightrope that he was walking it seemed to me that perhaps a scriptural answer would be most tactful. I cast about for a moment and then came up with one.

"Do you remember in the Bible when Joseph was wandering among the Shechemites? One of the Shechemites saw him and asked him a question. Do you remember what it was?"

The pastor thought. "He asked, 'Whom are you seeking?'"

"And Joseph's answer?"

"He said, 'I seek my brethren.'"

"Well that," I said, "is my answer to your question too."[2]

2

The Most Aggressive Means

No one needed to be convinced about the effectiveness of using radio to communicate messages as World War II was winding down. In Europe and the United States, radio in the early '40s meant listening to the powerful voice of Edward R. Murrow broadcasting from the rooftops of buildings during bombing raids or from locations made into vivid mental pictures during that war. There were more than 1,000 radio stations on the air in the United States during this time, and nearly 90 percent of families in the U.S. had radio sets in their homes.

What did people get from radio around the world during that time? News in a more immediate manner, as in the case of Murrow and other wartime reporters; entertainment in the form of music and quiz shows; and escape during the day by serial dramas that were, at least in the United States, sponsored by soap companies. They were the first soap operas. People from all cultural, social, and economic levels tuned in daily to the events of each day's fiction. But they didn't always consider it fiction, for when a script would involve a character having a baby, notes of congratulation along with baby gifts poured in to the stations from all corners. The same would occur if there was mention of anniversaries or birthdays in the scripts. If characters were destitute, offers of money flowed in.

Researchers who studied audiences of radio programs showed that people listened for the following reasons: escape from monotony, disappointment, or difficulty; provision of guidance and moral values in family and interpersonal matters; bolstering of self-esteem; companionship; and entertainment. People were, in effect, getting counseling from soap operas!

The Church of the Nazarene was looking into how to use radio to spread the gospel during the same time period. At the 1944 General Assembly in the Municipal Auditorium in Minneapolis, discussion centered on how powerful a medium radio was and what role it could play in reaching people for Christ. The minutes of that assembly show that while "the founders of our church saw the importance of the printed page . . . and established a publishing house to be operated under the supervision of the church, and since radio has become a medium of promotion equal to, if not greater than the printed page, and is of unlimited possibilities . . ." the church was asked to pursue the medium as a way to spread the gospel.

In a message to the Nazarene Young People's Society at that assembly, Rev. Norman Oke (then general NYPS president) said that this was the time to concentrate on religious broadcasts, while radio was still in its infancy in religious programming. "I suggest a National Holiness Hour over a continent-wide chain of stations," he said. "What church has better music to draw from? Where would you find better preachers than the cream of our crop? We have the combination of talent and experience to produce a broadcast second to none . . .

"A Holiness Hour . . . would be one of the greatest single agencies since the Wesleyan Revival in shaking this continent with Wesley's world-shaking gospel. Holiness deserves just this." The assembly was convinced. On June 21 the wheels for a radio effort were set in motion with this resolution: "That the General Superintendents appoint a commission of five to study the question of radio work and report to the General Board, and that the General Board shall have the power to act."

Many present-day readers who have been on boards of various natures know what that kind of resolution can mean. The resolution asking for further study is sometimes a way to make the idea go away permanently, when there aren't enough No votes to put a stop to the idea in the first place.

But it is easy now to see that this commission of five was not a team assembled to put a plan out of its misery. As if radio were not a strong enough medium on its own, the commission members of M. A. Lunn, S. T. Ludwig, Selden Dee Kelley, Haldor Lillenas, and Merle Dimbath ensured the involvement of the Church of the Nazarene in radio. They gathered later in 1944, and by their second meeting on January 4, 1945, they had articulated the potential and problems of using radio that are still with us 50 years later. In that meeting there was unanimous agreement that, because of cost, "it is extremely difficult to break into the religious radio field now—and likely will not get any better." The commission also agreed that "the whole of religious broadcasting has suffered from bad programming."

"There is a place on the radio for adequate and well planned religious radio programs geared to a sort of tempo that will catch the listening audience," according to the minutes from that meeting. "There was practically unanimous agreement not only as to a place for such a program, but the need for it, provided it was properly sponsored."

The commission was keenly aware that if proper financing was not available, a different kind of cost would be incurred—by people turning off their radios, or, worse, tuning back to their soap operas.

"All agree that unless a good program can be put on, the cost of a cheap one would be too much," the minutes said. A sample program was prepared by Blair MacPhail of the Potts-Turnbull Advertising Agency, and an informal poll was taken regarding the name of the proposed program. Most were leaning toward the name "Showers of Blessing."

The commission members had caught the vision. They saw that no other medium at that time could carry the message with the reach and impact of radio. In their report to the General Board later that month, they said what remains true today: "There is unparalleled opportunity in the field of radio for gospel broadcasting. We believe we are faced, as a church, with a tremendous challenge to herald the gospel of full salvation by every means at our disposal . . .

"As an evangelistic agency the radio offers a most fertile field and toward the extension of the local church in every community, it can hardly be surpassed. Because of the *urgency* of our mission—Giving Christ to the Nations—and the *potency* of our message—Preaching Christ, the Savior of the World, we believe the radio furnishes the most aggressive means of getting the gospel to needy men and women who are untouched by the message of Christ and the church."

The commission recommended that the denomination immediately sponsor a coast-to-coast broadcast in the United States, and then around the world as soon as possible. The board liked what they heard. Two months later there was an organization called the Nazarene Radio League, with the tireless T. W. Willingham as its executive director. He chose Rev. Stanley Whitcanack to help him. By that summer, "Showers of Blessing" was on the air.

Great care was taken to combine, as Rev. Oke suggested, the denomination's strong music and preaching. The Orpheus Choir from Olivet Nazarene College, directed by Walter Larsen, traveled to Kansas City right after the school's commencement in June to record the music for the first eight programs. General Superintendent H. V. Miller was the program's first speaker.

Other programs during that year included the choir from Detroit First Church of the Nazarene, directed by Ray Moore. Moore later moved to Kansas City to be the program's music director. Twenty-seven different people spoke during the first year of the program, but the most frequent were Russell V. DeLong and L. A. Reed. The cost of putting on a weekly 30-minute program was estimated at nearly $300,000 per year.

In that first year, 37 radio stations in the United States carried the program. Within eight years there were nearly 400.

"The potency of radio as an instrument of public enlightenment has become increasingly obvious, until today its importance in this sphere is unchallengeable," Willingham said to the radio committee in the '50s. "Today it is possible to reach more people, faster, and more effectively by means of radio than by any other method."

But Willingham was keenly aware of what was needed to keep the gospel on the airwaves, much as the first commission was aware of what was necessary to make the venture worth starting. Listeners needed to hear a message worth hearing.

"This assumes that the message to be imparted is *sufficiently interesting* to command listener attention from those exposed to the message," Willingham continued, "and therein lies the greatest snag upon which so many fond hopes are wrecked in the business of radio broadcasting." He asked each committee member to commit this previous sentence to memory.

Willingham also tried to generate interest within the denomination to support the radio effort. The church's general fund could not cover the costs of the broadcasts and distribution, so he established a Radio League membership organization, where people could contribute $1.00 per month. If contributions and pledges did not come in, members received notes from Willingham, who, even in form letters, did not mince words.

After describing a situation in which a mission in another country desired to air "Showers of Blessing" but couldn't afford to, he appealed to league members in the U.S.

"These broadcasts on foreign soil have meant much to our missionaries and to our work," he wrote. "We have so many religious services here in the homeland and our struggling workers abroad have so few, it would seem almost sinful to deny them one short Nazarene program a week."

Then, in true Willingham style, he asked members: "What do you think we should do? Forget it, or do something about it?"

Willingham believed in the effort so much that when he went on his frequent revival trips as the preacher, he turned his honoraria over to the radio league.

"He didn't know any more effective way to get the Church of the Nazarene's name before the people than was possible with radio," said Clara Rogers, his secretary. "He just wanted to get a nugget of truth on the air."

During the early years, Willingham offered "Showers of Blessing" free to any station that would broadcast it on Palm Sunday and Easter. More than 700 stations participated.

"We had a lot of requests for transcripts of sermons," Rogers said. "Rev. DeLong had a knack for grabbing people's attention." Indeed, DeLong was a popular preacher. Before his 20 years with "Showers of Blessing" ended, he had delivered 773 radio messages.

But the cost of putting the program on the air continued to be a burden. In 1947 the 30-minute program was cut to 15 minutes because it was cheaper to buy less airtime, and more local churches could help sponsor shorter programs. The additional hope was that more nonchurch people would listen to the entire program if it were shorter.

In 1965 Willingham retired from his director's job, 20 years after being the Radio League's only leader. H. Dale Mitchell, former pastor of Detroit First Church of the Nazarene, succeeded him. In 1973 Paul Skiles became the director.

Rev. DeLong also felt he needed to retire. In 1968 C.

William Fisher was the main preacher for "Showers of Blessing," where he was featured for eight years. Other preachers on the program have included Earl Lee, Ponder Gilliland, Paul Cunningham, and Chuck Millhuff. Ray Moore and Gary Moore were music directors and engineers for the program for a combined 30 years.

Interest in a denomination-wide broadcast waned considerably in the '70s and '80s, though, and "Showers of Blessing" was taken off the air in 1984. It was replaced with "Masterplan," a broadcast with evangelist Stephen Manley, but it ended in 1988. Radio was not the dominant medium it was in the '40s and '50s for U.S. audiences, and support from local churches and the General Budget reflected that shift.

But some churches thought radio was still an effective way to communicate gospel messages to audiences. Phil Stout, an associate pastor at First Church of the Nazarene in Elkhart, Ind., and Jerry Brewton, an insurance agent in Elkhart, teamed up to produce their own program when the denomination's programs ended. Stout had worked for a local radio station and had also done five-minute reflective segments for the local church to air in conjunction with "Showers of Blessing" and "Masterplan."

When Stout became pastor of a Jackson, Mich., Nazarene church, he and Brewton continued to work on the program. It is a casual dialogue format interspersed with contemporary Christian music. Stout and Brewton discuss themes such as how people change—from the outside in or the inside out; having the joy of Christ throughout the year rather than just at holiday times; putting pain in perspective; and setting priorities so that daily calendars reflect people's values.

Approximately 30 radio stations in the U.S. air the program. It was also broadcast to troops in the Middle East during the Gulf War in 1991 by Trans World Radio from Cyprus. Now several English-speaking regions in Africa and the Far East air the program, and its base is growing.

World Mission Radio offerings cover the cost of the international transmissions, and individual churches and listeners cover the production costs with contributions.

The popularity of "Masterdesign" illustrates the universal nature of the gospel message when it is not tied to a particular nation or culture. During the Gulf War, for instance, when some religious groups said the military action was wrong, and others said it was right, Stout and Brewton tried to address a deeper issue in their broadcasts. Stout said that Jesus' approach to such matters was what they strived for.

"I'm reminded of the time a Roman centurion asked Jesus to heal his servant, and Jesus did," Stout said. "Some people wish Jesus had told the centurion to stop fighting after the servant was healed. Others wish Jesus had said to continue fighting. But He didn't do either. He just ministered to the guy."

And since there is a five-month delay from taping to broadcast, Brewton said it was difficult to keep up with current events.

"But life situations, relationships, and other problems —those things don't change," he said. "It doesn't matter if you're in Africa, America, or on a battlefield in the Persian Gulf."

Even though radio is not as popular in the U.S. as it used to be, the influence of the medium in other parts of the world continues to grow. In the early '50s it was clear that with the early success of "Showers of Blessing," and a knowledge that approximately half of the world's population spoke Spanish, a program for Spanish-speaking people was needed.

So many people felt the burden for a Spanish program that, despite no possible funding from the Radio League because of the cost of broadcasting "Showers of Blessing," different departments in the denomination coordinated to produce and fund the program. The Nazarene World Mission Society took responsibility for raising the money for the broadcast through a special offering each August. The first year's offering raised $11,000. Twenty years later it raised more than $150,000. Thirty-nine years later, nearly $700,000. The Spanish Department gave guidance in coaching the choir and provided the excellent preaching of Dr. H. T. Reza. The Nazarene Radio League produced the program, made the contacts with the stations, and supplied the stations with tapes of the broadcasts.

The first broadcast of "La Hora Nazarena" (The Nazarene Hour) was in June 1953 and was carried on 12 stations in Latin America. It followed a similar format of "Showers of Blessing" in that it had music and preaching. The music was a bit of a drawback for some listeners because it was clear that the singers in those early broadcasts were from North America singing in Spanish. Latin Americans, like most cultures, prefer to hear from their own people, and they take fierce pride in their own "sound." It is similar, as Paul Miller points out in his 1978 book *Stop, Look, and Listen,* to how a person from South Carolina would hear and use English different from someone in Australia. But the drawback was largely overshadowed by the powerful preaching of Reza, a Latin American himself, who was also editor of the denomination's Spanish publications and a familiar name to people of Latin America.

"The people liked Dr. Reza very much because his preaching was good and they knew he was one of them," said Howard Conrad, a former missionary to Cuba, Peru, and Costa Rica. "Reza saw things the Hispanic way. He preached from a context of understanding who the people were and how they made decisions—even spiritual decisions. While an Anglo might make a spiritual decision as an individual, the Hispanic way involves authority patterns where one discusses a decision with family members and it becomes a group process. Reza knew that and spoke with that understanding."

Reza also discussed issues that got to the heart of the matter in Hispanic cultures.

"He didn't get overly philosophical but would be very direct with topics such as witchcraft," said Conrad. "He was on their level in a clear, compassionate, yet direct way."

Almost immediately after it began, "La Hora Nazarena" was broadcast in Mexico, Ecuador, Guatemala, Nicaragua, Costa Rica, Panama, Colombia, and Venezuela.

"My goal for my sermons was to make them short and make them complete," said Reza. "I also knew that, to reach the diverse audience of South America, Central America, and elsewhere, I had to avoid all colloquial expressions, and concentrate on points 1, 2, and 3."

Reza's voice became so well known that it was not unusual for him to be in a public place in some remote part of the world and have a stranger approach him to ask if he had a radio program called "La Hora Nazarena."

"I was even in a heated discussion with an official at an airport, and a man interrupted the discussion to ask if I was Rev. Reza," he said. "The man was a pastor and listened to the program regularly. It was difficult to continue my heated discussion after that."

Conrad said that the popularity of Reza and the programs made his own task as a missionary easier, in part because the broadcasts were often people's first contact with the Church of the Nazarene. Some had already accepted Christ, and some were involved in home-study programs before they knew of a local church, Conrad said.

"One of the purposes for the program was to tell people that the Church of the Nazarene was available," said Reza. "La Hora Nazarena" quickly became the largest Protestant radio broadcast in the Spanish language. Conrad said it was also the only Nazarene program in Cuba allowed on the air by the island's leader, Fidel Castro.

In 1974 Dr. Reza retired as the program's preacher, after delivering more than 1,000 messages over the airwaves.

But while "Showers of Blessing" and "La Hora Nazarena" were reaching millions around the world in the late '60s, a completely different radio effort was taking place in the Cape Verde Islands, in the Atlantic Ocean between South America and Africa.

The islands were a Portuguese colony under the dictatorship of Antonio Salazar, and religious broadcasting on commercial stations was forbidden.

However, Jorge de Barros, a Nazarene pastor from the islands, had an interest in amateur radio and was part of a group of people with similar interests. He was unaware of the English and Spanish broadcasts being beamed around the world. At a Saturday night banquet for the amateur radio club members and their spouses, a gathering of the area's influential people, Barros was made president of their group.

"I laughed when I was made president because, as I told them, the next day I was having my pastoral vote," Barros said. "So while I was being given this job, it was possible I would be losing my other job."

The club members had never heard of this kind of election. His comment created such a stir that the next morning the local radio station was in the worship service broadcasting the service. In a dictatorial society, a vote is newsworthy. The station broadcast the singing and prayer, and the rest of the service that led up to the vote.

"I almost panicked because I wondered, What if I get a terrible vote? Everyone will hear about it," he said. "Luckily I had a 100 percent vote!" And the whole town knew about it.

A few weeks later Barros approached the same station and offered them an hour-long program at no charge, called "A Hora Nazarena" (The Nazarene Hour). The station accepted the offer, and Barros produced the program.

By the early '70s, Barros was sending copies of the program to Nazarene Headquarters in Kansas City, where they were processed, duplicated, and sent to other Portuguese-speaking countries. "A Hora Nazarena" became a popular program in Angola, Mozambique, Brazil, Portugal, and in the Azores. It played a role in establishing the Nazarene work in the Azores, because the people were already familiar with the church's name when the work began.

And since the Church of the Nazarene is only beginning work in Angola, the program has made a different kind of impact there. During a period of brutal terrorist attacks in that country, certain kinds of broadcasts were taken off the air. But one station wanted to broadcast something that would possibly calm the fears of the people.

They chose one of Barros's programs with his sermon, "The Prince of Peace." That message of Christ was delivered repeatedly day and night.

"The program made such an impact that a Catholic priest wrote to us and told us about the broadcast," Barros said.

He also remembers receiving a most unusual letter from a European businessman based in Angola. The man wanted to buy a cassette with two prayers on it.

"For months he had been listening to 'A Hora Nazarena,'" Barros said. "He decided to start a club, in his own living room, with the programs he had recorded. He gave it a special name, *Clube A Hora Nazarena* (The Nazarene Hour Club). Friends came regularly for the meetings. Now they had a problem. Could we sell them two prayers—one to open the club time and one to close it—'because no one here knows how to pray?'" At the present, several Portuguese-speaking districts are producing their own programs.

"I think local programs are healthy," Barros said. "They get the local support, and they train their own people. But it takes the right people with the drive to make it effective."

The goal for the Nazarene radio effort now is to continue to expand the number of programs produced in the different parts of the world. The more the broadcast sounds like a home-produced program, with references to local customs, holidays, issues, and in local dialect, the more credibility the program has. French broadcasts from Quebec, for instance, are not accepted well in French-speaking Haiti or France. Around the world people desire to hear programming from those who sound like their neighbors.

This introduces an enormous challenge to producing credible gospel messages worldwide. Training people in broadcast technology and programming practices takes a great deal of time and money. The expansion can occur only as training and financial support expands. There is need for people to help train and establish broadcasting studios in every region.

As it was 50 years ago, the intent of sending the gospel over airwaves is to bring the good news of salvation to those who have not yet met Jesus; to establish a link between churches and listeners; to bring listeners into a fellowship of believers; and to encourage those who are already believers.

In some parts of the world these objectives are being met with great success. Local programming has taken off, and the results are exciting. But what about other regions that are without the staff and technology, yet have people who need to hear the message? The question posed by T. W. Willingham, when faced with the challenge of people wanting to hear these messages, might apply: "What do you think we should do? Forget it or do something about it?"

3

The Vehicle That Joined Them Together

In 1967, after the United States invaded the Dominican Republic, Alfonso Ortega's father lost his government job with that country and was extremely depressed. Alfonso noticed that his father secluded himself in a room in the house to listen to the radio.

"No one knew what he was listening to, but after a few months we saw some gradual changes in the way he was acting," Alfonso said. "Then one night he announced that we were all going to listen to a radio program together." The program was "La Hora Nazarena," and Alfonso remembers the program's speaker, Dr. H. T. Reza, reading the words to the hymn:

> I gave My life for thee;
>   My precious blood I shed,
> That thou might'st ransomed be,
>   And quickened from the dead.
> I gave, I gave My life for thee.
> What has thou giv'n for Me?

"That night I felt something different about myself," Alfonso said. "I sensed that same touch two years later when I began attending the Nazarene church that had just opened in my town. Then my father asked me to pray with him. We both accepted Christ together. We became Christians because of 'La Hora Nazarena.'"

That program is the most famous of the Nazarene radio programs outside the United States and has been produced since 1953. H. T. Reza and Juan Vazquez-Pla were the primary speakers for 30 years, and their voices became identified with holiness and the Church of the Nazarene throughout the Spanish-speaking world.

Since 1981 "La Hora Nazarena" has been produced in Costa Rica at the center for Nazarene Communications in Latin America (Comunicaciones Nazarenas Latinoamericanas, or COMUNAL) on the grounds of the Nazarene Seminary of the Americas in San Jose. It is still produced in its traditional form, with a hymn and a sermon, but, with 50 percent of Latin America under the age of 20, a more contemporary format was added in an attempt to reach younger audiences. The new format includes dramatizations of biblical lessons, along with dialogues between Giovanni Monterroso and Mauricio Valverde. Monterroso, a missionary from Guatemala, was COMUNAL's director from 1987 to 1992, and Valverde, a Costa Rican layman who has a seminary degree as well as a university degree in journalism, is assistant director. Monterroso said every other religious radio program in Latin America followed the format of a hymn and a sermon. To reach those who weren't listening, he said, something different had to be offered.

"There is a principle in mass communications that listeners identify with either speakers or with programs," he said. "Most people who knew of 'La Hora Nazarena' identified with the speaker. They identified the Church of the Nazarene with either Reza or Vazquez-Pla. That's typical of mass communication.

"When I came I thought it was time the listener should identify with the program, not the person. Because when they identify with the person and the person leaves, then the identity is shaky. I wanted people to link the program more directly with the church."

The dialogue format gives equal importance to Monterroso and Valverde, and the music is more aligned with Latin American culture.

"No other religious program was doing this," Monterroso said. "One of the criticisms of the traditional programs was that the music was too solemn and that it was sung by North Americans. Its effect was to edify people who were already Christians. Our purpose with the new program was to reach the non-Christian or the person who had recently accepted Christ, and to reach younger people." Both formats address holiness, but the new format does so by showing holiness in action through the dramas and dialogues on themes such as family problems, friendships, ecology, and dating.

"The traditional 'La Hora Nazarena' was explicitly identified as the international voice of the Church of the Nazarene," Monterroso said. "Latin American Nazarenes believed the program should be for them. I think there should also be a program where Nazarenes talk to nonbelievers. As a result, most of the people who write us are not Nazarenes or believers but are people who want to know more about our topics on the program."

The new format was instrumental in leading Henri and Jeanna Torres to Christ in 1991. Jesus Espinoza, a seminary student from Peru who also works at COMUNAL, was going door-to-door in a San Jose neighborhood, telling people that the Church of the Nazarene would soon be opening in the area. When he knocked on the Torres's door, it was "like having someone falling from the sky with advanced training in theology," said Henri. "For a long time I had wanted to know more about the Bible."

Espinoza left cassettes of "La Hora Nazarena" with the Torreses, and told them when the program would be on in their area. They listened, and soon Espinoza was conducting Bible studies in their home. He eventually led them to Christ.

"I was impressed with the technical quality of the cassettes," Henri said. "It was an incentive to listen to the program on the radio. Many programs have good technique, but this one had good technique and good content."

Jeanna said that the programs that dealt with friendships were of particular value to her.

"They made me analyze my own friendships and reflect on the kinds of relationships I develop," she said. "Besides, the music is precious."

Henri said the friendship programs changed the way he treated his friends and showed him how Christ was his friend.

"I saw that I could go to Christ for advice—go to Him as a friend. And the music repeatedly communicated how to know Christ."

Some of the programs were reenactments of Christ's parables. Henri said he had never heard the parable of the sower before.

"It was presented as a drama, and I understood its meaning. It illustrated the importance for having good roots in Christ so that you won't slip away."

Jeanna added, "It also showed that the sower needs to know where to sow where it will bear fruit."

Both say they are different because of their relationship with Christ.

"I feel more optimistic and more tranquil," said Henri. "Life is better."

Jeanna said that her new relationship with Christ has made her want to do something for others.

"I have tried to be kind, but since knowing Christ in this new way I want to help others and I sense God directing me that way. Growing up I helped my school raise money to help orphans. The desire to help has increased since then. Now that we know Christ, I am praying that God will open the doors to help me see where I can minister."

Espinoza saw firsthand how effective radio can be in developing a ministry. "The radio programs were an evangelistic outreach that grew into neighborhood Bible study," he said. "It was a way to get started. It will help me as a pastor, too, because if the church does dramas or kids' ministries, I can do that because of my experience at COMUNAL."

Espinoza also experienced God's power through radio as a result of a drama he wrote for a program. While preparing to write a script for a recent "La Hora Nazarena" on the theme of the miracles of Christ, he remembered how his grandfather had been healed of Parkinson's disease at an evangelistic crusade in Peru.

"The preacher prayed for the healing of those in the audience," Espinoza said. "My grandfather started to pray also, with his hands shaking uncontrollably. But by the end of the prayer his hands slowly stopped moving. He was healed. I had heard about this kind of healing, but I had never seen it for myself."

Espinoza said that he wanted to write about that incident for the radio drama, since it affected him so deeply. After the script was written and rehearsed, it was time to put it on the air. Normally the group stops for prayer before the recording session begins, but this day they forgot.

"Just before the recording began, Giovanni remembered, and said God might use this program to heal someone listening," Espinoza said.

"Two weeks after the program was broadcast, we got a letter from Lima, Peru, not far from where my grandfather was healed, and the writer said his vision was healed as he prayed during the prayer in the drama. It was the power of God through the radio."

The communications effort in Latin America has come a long way from its original office in 1981, in a small space upstairs of the church on the seminary grounds. The idea of that office was a novel one; it was an effort to decentralize the radio effort that came from Kansas City, where "La Hora Nazarena" had been recorded and distributed. Juan Vazquez-Pla was teaching at the seminary, and the experiment of producing a radio program took shape. A new communications building with offices and recording facilities was built in 1985 by Work and Witness teams.

The office received approximately 15 letters a week from listeners to its new program in 1981. Now they receive more than 100 letters a week and produce eight different programs. COMUNAL staffers also train four seminary students per year to answer letters from listeners, to write, record, and edit radio programs, and show them how to use a radio ministry in their own countries. Having representatives from several countries working in the office helps keep the themes of the programs current with the cultures and concerns of the countries. The arrangement also creates a network of pastors throughout Latin America who continue to utilize radio ministries in their own geographic areas. Those in the training program receive scholarships that substantially reduce their seminary tuition.

In addition to the two styles of "La Hora Nazarena," COMUNAL produces:

"Something New for Today"—designed for the believer, this 15-minute program presents Bible studies and conferences by outstanding Nazarene preachers.

"Confronting Your Destiny"—a five-minute daily program targeted to the non-Christian who is indifferent to the gospel. It uses themes that relate to daily realities and problems, with the goal to meet sinners where they are.

"German's Airwaves"—a program of Christian rock music that provides the lyrics in both Spanish and English to listeners who write requesting them. The program is sponsored by local churches on secular radio stations and provides an opportunity for friendship evangelism, since the local churches take responsibility for personal contact and follow-up of letters.

"Life Is like This"—a five-minute daily program for the Christian that focuses on themes of daily living such as family relations, salvation by faith, death, and gossip. The topics are presented in a drama format, making the program particularly popular.

"Our Marvelous World"—designed for children, this program uses dramatizations by animal characters to present scientific information with a spiritual application.

"We Are Alive"—to be used as public service announcements during times of public crises such as earthquakes, floods, or other disasters. Each is 45 seconds long, designed to provide emotional support to disaster victims. They are written with the help of a psychologist, and every district superintendent has them for immediate distribution when the need arises.

"Spots That Impact"—vary from 15 to 60 seconds, these spots promote the gospel and its ideals.

Women's Programs—one-minute daily spots that feature themes for the 25- to 35-year-old woman who is not a believer. They air on secular stations as public service announcements.

Video Dramas—stories of people who have found Christ are reenacted in a drama, with the testimony of the actual subject at the end.

In 1989 COMUNAL sent a survey to radio stations that used their programs, to district superintendents throughout Latin America, and to a sampling of listeners who had written to programs. The objective of the survey was to get a demographic profile of who was listening. The survey had a response rate of almost 50 percent, which is very high for similar studies.

Sixty-five percent of the listeners were men, 62 percent were between 20 and 29 years of age, 75 percent said they had been listening for three years or fewer, and 13 percent said they listened to the programs with eight or more people. Among the district superintendents, 75 percent said the programs were broadcast in their districts, and half of the local churches supported the programs through radio offerings.

Another objective was to find out attitudes about design and content of programs. Nearly 90 percent of listeners were positive; 85 percent of the superintendents were positive, and 64 percent of the radio stations responding were positive, especially in regard to the music. For the dialogue and drama format of "La Hora Nazarena," 100 percent of the stations were positive, because the majority of other religious programs they aired were strictly sermons and hymns.

An important result of the survey showed that the variety of accents in the programs were not a problem to listeners. The accents were different because the people of COMUNAL come from so many different Latin American countries. But the listeners accepted those accents because they were still Latin American accents, and the cultures of those countries are so similar. The acceptance level goes down considerably if the accent is from North America.

Eighty-seven percent of listeners said the themes of the programs applied to their daily living, while 93 percent said the programs had helped them with their spiritual growth and encouraged them to share their faith. All superintendents said their districts had benefited from the programs.

Some of the comments on the surveys returned by superintendents are: "Church growth has been notable especially in rural areas where TV has no influence. Thanks to 'La Hora Nazarena,' we have organized two churches with people who regularly listen to the program."

"'La Hora Nazarena' is helpful in presenting the doctrine of the church. The other programs are good resources for ideas and activities in the churches."

All of these programs carry a message at their conclusion that they were sponsored by the Church of the Nazarene, and they invite letters addressed to COMUNAL. Listeners who write in response to programs are sent information on correspondence courses, such as "Biblical Basis for My Growth in Christ." That course includes seven lessons on topics such as the Christian home, how to walk with God, and baptism. Another course of six lessons is "Biblical Basis of Holiness." More than 1,000 have enrolled in the courses. Those taking the courses complete one lesson at a time, send it to COMUNAL for comments and correction, and then are sent the next lesson in the series.

The person who now oversees correspondence with listeners is German Picavea, from Argentina, who was one of the first seminary students to be trained at COMUNAL. Some of the letters are responding to offers made at the end of some programs for free gifts, such as calendars, key chains, and booklets. Some ask for prayers, Bible study courses, or advice; some just are greetings from listeners.

But most are letters that German says he can't classify because they are "special."

"I open the mail from the perspective of a pastor," he said. "A letter reflects the person, not a piece of paper."

He said that in the Latin American culture a letter is a very important thing because typically people don't write to one another, even if loved ones are away from each other. So high value is put on a letter when it comes because it shows high desire on that person's part and a favorable disposition toward the program. It requires a lot of effort not only to write but also to send the letter. In many places it means the person has to go downtown, which can take a whole day. Then, a stamp can be expensive. In Argentina a stamp costs about $1.00 U.S.; many people in that country make around $100 U.S. per month. German estimates that each letter represents 5,000 people.

If a letter is as simple as asking how to become a Christian, the person is sent a plan of salvation and is encouraged to find a church. Everyone who writes receives a Bible correspondence lesson. If the people write back, they are sent more lessons that take them to the point of asking Christ into their lives, being baptized, and becoming church members.

German also writes to other religious programs that are on the air to see if they respond to letters. "I like to compare how we operate to the other programs," he said. "Very few respond."

Most of the letters he receives from listeners ask for more information about the theme of a particular program or specific aspects of the Bible. Many write because they sense they can get help from the producers of these programs. One letter writer said that after hearing a program about jealousy, he thought the voices on the radio were talking directly to him. The program helped him think about his attitude, so he wrote to find out more about changing his jealous feelings.

"Because of the details people tell us about themselves, you can tell that they have been touched by God through these programs," German said.

The program "Confronting Your Destiny" receives the most letters from Cuba, where listeners pick up the broadcast over shortwave radio. Approximately 50 letters per month come from listeners in that country who ask for prayer for the political situation and for the suffering in that country. Many letters ask for Bibles.

"You can tell there is a paper shortage in Cuba because we get notes on very narrow strips of rough paper, pieces of bags, anything they can find to write on," German said.

He looks for two things in following up on letters written to COMUNAL. The first is that he tries to look beyond what is written.

"I count on the Holy Spirit to help me see beyond the statement, 'My husband doesn't love me any more,' or 'My children don't obey me,'" he said. The second thing is that he encourages each writer to go to a local pastor for help. He has written a manual for pastors and district superintendents to see how the follow-up can work in their cities.

The ideal is that COMUNAL works in concert with local churches, and the clearest example of how effective it can be was in November 1989, when Georgina Herrara from Ecuador wrote after hearing "La Hora Nazarena."

"I am 37 years old and work in a textile factory and have three children," she wrote. "I am writing to you because last night I turned on the radio to listen to whatever program in order to forget my problems for a few minutes. By chance I turned on 'La Hora Nazarena,' and since you said we could write to you, I am writing to ask your help, which I desperately need. In my desperation I have been considering killing myself and my three teenagers. I am not a Christian and have not taught my children about God. Maybe that is why God is punishing me now. Please help me, as I live in a home that has no happiness."

COMUNAL forwarded the letter to Daniel Pesado, the pastor of the Nazarene church in her town. Pesado had recently attended the Seminary of the Americas and was well aware of how important COMUNAL programs were. The church was just a few blocks from Georgina's home. Some of her problems were with her husband, she said a year later in an interview.

"He was no longer interested in me or the children," she said. "He beat me and the children and was gone frequently. We had a life with no life. There were many moments when I wanted to take my life and my children's lives just to get us away from this. That's when I heard 'La Hora Nazarena' and wrote the letter."

As soon as Pesado got the note from COMUNAL, he went to the home. Georgina's husband answered the door. He was angry that a man had come calling for his wife.

"I was afraid that because my husband was so violent, he might hurt the pastor," Georgina said. "So I told the pastor I couldn't talk then. He invited me to church."

Georgina and her son, Frankie, went to the church, and when people were invited to come forward and accept Christ, Frankie went forward. Georgina's daughter, Tatiana, attended church with them the next Sunday and began her journey with Christ that day. Three months later, Georgina found Christ.

"We didn't see changes in our home overnight,"

Georgina said. "But God gave us a most important gift—peace in our souls. I can't say that God gave us riches and solved all of our problems, but I thank God that I have two beautiful children who know how to pray. There is peace and happiness in my home."

Georgina's husband has moved out of the house, and the family is praying for his salvation.

"Maybe by a person, or a church, or a radio, my father will find Christ," said Tatiana. "God provided radio as the instrument for us to find Him."

Pesado said he was humbled to be part of the process that eventually brought three of the Herraras to Christ.

"But the difference in this family was a radio program," he said. "In this family it was the vehicle that joined them together with life. And this is just one family in the world. There are millions more with desperate needs, considering suicide, experiencing the personal problems Georgina had."

4

Stories Tell the Story

To get to the home of Jorge and Cecelia Solis, one must get off the road at the crest of a hill in a remote section of San Jose, Costa Rica, and walk between deteriorating houses down a steep path of dirt and rocks. During the rainy season the path is barely passable, as is the narrow wooden bridge that crosses a deep canyon. Next to the bridge is a metal tub where they wash their clothes. A hose draws the water up from the creek in the canyon.

Jorge built the house—a one-room A-frame with a wood-burning iron stove, a table, two beds, chairs, couch, and electrical outlet. They have a goat. Outside and inside are songbirds Jorge has caught and placed in bamboo cages, and the birds fill the air with notes from all octaves. The grounds surrounding the house are covered with purple, orange, burgundy, yellow, white, and blue flowers. He's a gardener. And he's got a temper.

Frustrated one day with the glasses that kept slipping down his face while trying to sign some papers, he crushed them. In another incident, while struggling with three policemen trying to arrest him for being disorderly, he knocked several teeth out of one. Cecelia was rightfully afraid of him.

There's one more thing in his house. There's a radio. When he couldn't sleep at night, which was frequently, he'd listen to it.

One of Jorge's gardening jobs is at the home of Bob

and Norma Brunson, who teach at the Seminary of the Americas. On an afternoon in 1991 Jorge and Bob were looking across the Brunsons' backyard, watching a menacing-looking storm develop over the mountains, heading their way.

Jorge mentioned that the approaching storm frightened him.

"Not me," said Bob in a casual manner. "I'm ready to go."

Bob's lack of anxiety bothered Jorge so much that he wondered about it for weeks. Jorge knew that he was not ready, he said later. He began listening more intently to the religious radio programs, including "La Hora Nazarena." He kept hearing offers of Bibles for those who wrote to the programs, but he was limited in reading and writing. And without his glasses, both were even more difficult. Finally he asked Norma why Bob felt that he was ready to die and wasn't afraid.

"I told him about the eternal life we have in Christ and asked him if he wanted it too," Norma said, in a matter-of-fact manner. Over the next several days she showed him passages of the Bible that told of God's love for us and the promise of eternal life.

Between what he had been hearing on the radio, and the personal touch of the Brunsons, Jorge knew he wanted Christ in his life.

"We knelt right there in the house, and he asked Christ to forgive him of his sins," Norma said. "It was unbelievable."

Jorge says that now he has contentment inside him where there once was turmoil. "If someone tells me they can't pay me today, I tell them it's OK and throw myself a psalm," he said.

Cecelia also became a believer when she heard a message on the radio that explained how to pray to accept Christ. She prayed the prayer along with the preacher.

"Jorge and I were both having problems with our tempers and in our marriage," she said. "We heard a message that said we should be praying together. We started doing that, and now things are in God's hands."

Norma meets with them weekly, using Bible lessons from COMUNAL. Jorge started inviting friends to the study, but for the most part they are suspicious of his new faith.

"It's like serenading a mule, trying to talk to them about Christ," he said.

Around the world there are stories of personal victory such as Jorge's, Cecelia's, and those mentioned in the previous chapter, where radio and personal contact were combined for a miraculous result. There are other kinds of victories, too, that have resulted in the starting of churches, using the same combination. Consider the following:

● A Guatemalan man was in charge of the group of people who taught catechism for the Catholic church in his city. He came to the Nazarene pastor in the area and wanted to know more about the Church of the Nazarene because he had been listening to the radio programs. He has since started a Church of the Nazarene with 45 catechism leaders, motivated by what they had been hearing.

● Before the Nazarene work was opened in Venezuela, Cecilia Rodriguez wrote, "I like your programs and I like your message, but you don't have a church here." William Porter visited her in December 1981. She gave him valuable suggestions about starting services in her community, and the work began in 1982.

Riding on a bus in Valencia, Venezuela, to meet with more radio contacts, Porter struck up a conversation with a man named Evaristo. The man told Porter of his close contacts with the dominant church. "Do these contacts help you feel close to God?" Porter asked. "No; in no way," was the reply. A few miles down the road Evaristo accepted Christ—the first convert in Venezuela.

"In my 30 years of missionary work, I have never seen a country so responsive to gospel radio broadcasts as in

Venezuela," said Porter. "In a small, remote community, an elderly lady told me how much she likes listening to the broadcasts. And also, in the great cities, the broadcast is heard." The best identification for the Church of the Nazarene in Venezuela is to be known as the church that sponsors "La Hora Nazarena."

● In Ecuador, several works in the jungle were started with the help of radio broadcasts. "La Hora Nazarena" was part of the program, followed by a message from the district superintendent. The broadcasts reached tribes of people who had never heard the gospel. Some of the programs dealt with unemployment, poverty, lack of food or education, and addressed some of the solutions to those problems. People got in contact with the superintendent for more information and instruction on how to start their own churches. Since the villages were difficult to reach in person, the superintendent's broadcasts would then address the needs mentioned in those contacts.

● In the Dominican Republic, representatives from the Church of the Nazarene tried to buy land to build a church. There was a particular area that was an ideal location, but the landowner refused the offer repeatedly. Somehow in the conversation the Church of the Nazarene was mentioned. The owner asked if this was the same group that sponsored "La Hora Nazarena." "Oh, I've heard of you," she said, and sold them the land.

● A student at the seminary received mass communication training from COMUNAL and has since returned to his home in Ecuador. He is using letters from listeners in Ecuador to help start churches there.

● In Riobamba, in the mountains of Ecuador, a man wrote that he had been listening to "La Hora Nazarena" and wanted to know more about the Church of the Nazarene. John Hall, who was getting a Bible school started in that country at the time, wrote the man and told him the church was just getting started in Ecuador. The man wrote back a few months later and said he had started a church in his home, and he invited Hall for a visit. Soon the congregation was too big for his home, so he rented a store for a meeting place.

A teenage girl from Riobamba accepted Christ at the church, and the action so enraged her father that he attempted to beat her to death. The Nazarene pastor took her into his home, and she eventually led her parents to Christ. She attended the seminary in Costa Rica, and now she and her husband are pastoring a church in Ecuador.

● When Larry and Eunice Bryant first opened the Church of the Nazarene in El Salvador in 1964, a family began attending because they had been hearing about the doctrine of holiness from Dr. Reza on "La Hora Nazarena." They said they wanted to know more and that they were "coming as hungry sheep," the Bryants said. The writings on holiness of W. T. Purkiser and H. Orton Wiley had not yet been translated into Spanish, so Eunice Bryant translated them so that the doctrines could be explained. At one session the father, Miguel Mejia, said, "Let's put aside the theology and see what the Bible says."

Miguel became a prominent layman in the church and felt a calling to put his business training to use at the newly organized seminary in Costa Rica. He was the school's first business manager, and he put a sizable amount of his salary from his business into scholarships. Miguel is retired now, but his son is the seminary's current business manager.

● Gabriel Lopez, from southeast Mexico, was 14 when his cousin invited him to come over to his house to study. His cousin was a Nazarene, but Gabriel's immediate family was Catholic. While studying, the cousin turned on the radio so they could listen to "La Hora Nazarena," with Dr. Reza preaching.

"My cousin said he wanted to be a radio announcer and sound like Reza, but I told him he was setting his sights too high," Gabriel said. "What I liked was the quartet music."

After high school Gabriel hitchhiked around Mexico for a few months. He remembers a specific rainy night when he couldn't find a ride or a place to stay, after six hours of walking.

"I laid down along the side of the road, and for the first time I was afraid," he said. "After two hours of torrential rain, I remembered a message from 'La Hora Nazarena' about how God loved me. I told God that if He would save me from this situation I would serve Him."

Three years after his promise to God, Gabriel had a dream that he was falling into an abyss. During the dream, as he was falling, he remembered Reza's message that God loved him. In his dream he called out to God and stopped falling. The next morning he was restless and disturbed by the dream, so he went to a pastor for help, but the pastor was out. He tried to find his cousin but couldn't. He walked past the Church of the Nazarene and saw that the door was open. He walked in and the pastor led him to Christ.

Later that week Gabriel had another dream, this time that he was dressed in a white robe, preaching to a large congregation. He asked the Nazarene pastor what it meant, and the pastor told him to wait and pray. Three days later the dream was repeated, as was the pastor's advice. Then it happened again. When the pastor suggested that this might be a call for Gabriel to preach, it caused great conflict in the family.

"My father was angry and said he would not help me pay to go to school," Gabriel said. "The church was having a youth camp and paid for me to go. I heard a message about God's call, and there I felt affirmed that my dreams were God calling me to preach."

He became a Nazarene pastor, then got a degree at the seminary in Costa Rica, while working at COMUNAL. He said it was possible for others to find God today by means of radio, just as it helped him.

● Rolando Giron, from western Guatemala, is another

student being trained at COMUNAL. He listens to music and types the lyrics into one of the computers so that certain songs can be matched with certain kinds of programs. He is finishing his master's degree at the seminary and pastors a church in the Costa Rican province of Limon.

In the early 1980s, when Giron was pastoring in his home country, five different groups of people contacted the district superintendent and asked how they could become Churches of the Nazarene. The groups were in northern Guatemala, a region not accessible by automobile. The district superintendent asked Rolando to accompany him to the area. It was a difficult trip into the jungle, but when they arrived they discovered congregations of 100 and more that had organized on the basis of listening to "La Hora Nazarena." By listening to the radio broadcasts together they had become congregations.

Rolando visited the villages for a week and performed 20 marriages, baptized 50 babies, and led 50 people to Christ. The district superintendent gave the congregations church status and helped the congregations elect a member to be pastor.

The superintendent had been broadcasting "La Hora Nazarena" for 15 minutes of his regular 30-minute radio program and answering letters or questions the other 15 minutes, so he was able to use that time to continue to give guidance to those new congregations over the airwaves.

In 1983, when Rolando was pastor of a different church in Guatemala, an independent group visited the superintendent and said they wanted to know more about the Church of the Nazarene because they had been hearing about it on "La Hora Nazarena." They even had a chapel that they used for worship. What they lacked was a leader. The superintendent asked Rolando to pastor that church as well, and in the first service, 20 people joined the church.

While he was pastoring those two churches, a family from a village several hours away by bus visited one of his services on a Sunday morning. They told him that they used to have a church in their village, but their pastor disappeared and people stopped attending. But some of the families had been listening to "La Hora Nazarena" and heard the district superintendent mention that Rolando was pastoring a new church in the same region, so they wanted to attend that church. The next Sunday more came to his church. Some of them accepted Christ that day.

"It didn't seem right for them to travel that far to come to church, so I decided to visit their village," Rolando said. "The man who originally came opened up his home for a meeting place, and I talked to the people about starting a church there. There were 20 people from the original church at that meeting."

Within a year the church was presented to the district assembly with 48 members. Soon it had its own pastor.

"It's a fact that radio opens doors to ministry," Rolando said. "I have seen it help start churches, and I have seen it through the letters we get at COMUNAL. I plan to use it to open doors and start churches when I am finished with school."

● Nehemias Rivera was 10 years old when he first heard "La Hora Nazarena" in the Andes region of Peru. His village was so remote that the pastor only visited once a year. But a congregation formed, and the leaders wrote outlines of the messages from the radio and then delivered them to the congregation as sermons. The hymns and choruses from the programs were used in the church services as well.

"I learned a lot about the gospel through radio," he said.

Despite this background, Nehemias didn't feel any ties to radio ministry until he was a work-study seminary student at COMUNAL.

"I had always felt radio ministry was distant—someone else's work," he said. "But now I am convinced that using radio is part of the complete pastoral work. I can prepare a sermon for Sunday and preach it to 50 to 100 people, but I can also broadcast it to thousands more over the airwaves."

We know that nothing by itself can start a church. It takes the movement of God and the willingness of people to lead and be led, it takes resources, and it takes need. In each of these examples above, it was radio that helped create a church or a pastor. The Church of the Nazarene now operates throughout Latin America in part because people heard the gospel by radio and were contacted by people who could tell them more.

One of the ways the radio effort is kept potent is through a prayer and support chain. There are 180 groups in 15 Latin American countries that are committed to supporting the radio efforts. Similar to the early Radio League days in the '40s in the U.S., the groups commit themselves to pray for the broadcasts, to listen to them and encourage others to listen, and to give offerings to help keep the programs on the air.

Jairo Montero, a seminary student from Venezuela, writes to each group every month to share prayer requests from listeners, share testimonies, and give information for when the broadcasts can be heard in that group's area.

"The groups are like a motor that keeps spreading the influence of the ministry," Montero said.

As the communications effort evolves, the goal is to continue to provide quality radio programming and to expand the ministry into video production. Radio is still the dominant medium in Latin America, as nearly everyone has access to radios and not as many have access to televisions. But that situation is temporary.

"The vision that the Church of the Nazarene had 50 years ago about radio now needs to include television and video," said Giovanni Monterroso, COMUNAL director. "Eventually those two media will complement radio in influence in Latin America, as it has in other parts of the world."

Adjacent to the COMUNAL office is a building under

construction that will house a television studio and video production facilities, along with classrooms for communications studies available to seminary students. That building was started by a Work and Witness team from four churches in Missouri. The COMUNAL budget cannot absorb construction costs of this new facility, so the next stage of development depends on when the next Work and Witness team can come. Through early 1993, five teams are scheduled to appear. The estimate for how many are needed is 12.

The teams from Missouri were so moved by the efforts of COMUNAL that they sent $3,000 after they returned to the U.S. to help finish the foundation before the rainy season began. When the new building is ready for use, the seminary will be able to offer students a certificate in communications.

"We need to be training more of our pastors in the use of mass communications," said COMUNAL's assistant director, Mauricio Valverde. "Training four at a time in our office is good, but if we could offer training to the entire seminary, they could return to their home countries and use the media as a tool for ministry with a local context."

Giving more pastors more mass media tools is a priority at COMUNAL.

"The pastor *has* to use these tools if he is going to be successful in the 20th century," said staffer German Picavea. "We help expand their vision and train them in the basics."

Monterroso said that there is an economic angle to this priority as well.

"Training a person in how to use the mass media is a better return on the money invested in the student, because that person will go to his or her own country and produce programs of local flavor that are specific to local need," he said. "If we are going to reach people, this kind of training is of ultimate importance. The international programs have their place, but local programs are more effective. The church is then investing in distinctive languages and cultures."

The training that seminary students will receive will not make them professionals in mass communication, but it is designed for pastors and laymen committed to using mass media in their ministry. Monterroso hopes that eventually the seminary will be able to offer a degree in communications. He believes support for this effort should come more and more from Latin American churches—the home territory—and less from North American churches.

"As we support our teachers and ministers, we need to recognize the use of mass media as a ministry also," he said.

Another goal is to establish these kinds of communications training centers where the denomination has Bible schools. Staffers would train people who would then go back to their cities and could put their training to use as a tool for ministry. Already the COMUNAL staff has produced manuals for starting radio ministries, using proper pronunciations, and developing follow-up programs for listeners who write to the studios. Members of the staff have traveled throughout Latin America to give workshops and seminars on radio and video ministries. Workshops have been conducted in Colombia, Argentina, Bolivia, and Mexico. Currently COMUNAL serves as a recording studio for Latin American musicians and also helps train groups in drama and puppet and clown ministries.

The services provided by COMUNAL are limited by financial realities and other inhibiting factors. Costs to finish the video wing of the building, produce several kinds of programs, distribute them to many countries, and train others in how to use the mass media are very high and easily exceed what is raised in the annual worldwide radio offering—the largest source of income.

A lack of money keeps programs from getting on stations that would reach more listeners. Religious stations broadcast the programs for free. With that arrangement, though, the station decides what time to air the program, and it might be at an inconvenient time for listeners. Airtime must be purchased for the longer programs on secular stations, at a prohibitive cost; but those stations will broadcast public service announcements at no charge, and COMUNAL's health and emergency spots are used in that framework.

An additional constraint is that evangelicals do not have a particularly good name in Latin America, because of fanatical groups that have come and gone—some that even paid poor villagers to attend church. Also, there remains Catholic opposition to evangelistic programming, which is one of the reasons it is so important to keep producing these programs.

"I am convinced that radio is a tool that God is using and will utilize in order that Nazarenes can take the message of salvation and holiness to the Spanish-speaking world that, after 500 years of Christianity, still needs to know Christ," Monterroso said.

Technical limitations exist too. Many areas do not have a local religious radio station, so listeners must use shortwave transmissions of powerful stations such as HCJB in Quito, Ecuador, or the Trans World Radio network. If a person is fortunate enough to have a shortwave radio, the times of the transmissions may not be conducive to listening. In addition, some churches oppose the programs aimed at reaching nonbelievers and won't support the programs on the local stations. Deviations from the traditional format of a hymn and a sermon are met with great resistance in some areas.

Still, the realization among pastors who have witnessed mass media ministry is clear. Proper use of radio can enhance virtually any ministry effort.

"If the opportunity presents itself for me to use radio, I'll be prepared," said Jairo Montero. "I know what is involved in follow up and in what is needed to use radio effectively."

Gabriel Lopez, who found Christ in part because of "La Hora Nazarena," said radio can still be used to change lives in much the same way it changed his.

"There are a lot of kids like me who now have Walkmans and are working in factories," he said. "They could be helped if they heard the message that God loved them, as I did. The message today needs to be in more of a style that young people would pay attention to. The newer programs talk about real life problems of today.

"Also, Christians need to be more involved in inviting people to listen to the programs with them, as my cousin did," he said. "At COMUNAL I learned to use communications to reach people who can't be reached another way. For instance, I learned how to write a script so that it would be acceptable to a radio audience."

Nehemias Rivera, another seminary student who has worked at COMUNAL, emphatically believes that, by means of radio, doors are opened and people receive help.

"This has awakened in me an awareness that, no matter what culture or country people are from, the basic needs are the same," he said. "Deep within each of us is an emptiness that needs to be filled with hope. I'm seeing how radio can be a part of the pastor's work to communicate that hope."

5

An Explosion of Interest

The world was transfixed at the sight in China that was displayed on television screens in June 1989. Millions of young people were gathering in Tiananmen Square, demanding a change in how they were being governed, calling for freedom for the citizenry. Many were fainting from the hunger strikes, the heat, or the press of the crowd. Mikhail Gorbachev, the Soviet leader, was due in Beijing for a visit with China's leaders. The timing was perfect for freedom and openness to be discussed within the government's walls and the public's squares.

Then came the tanks. Unarmed civilians stood in front of them, forcing the drivers either to stop or to crush the people standing in their way. The collective will of the protesters brought the might of the military to a grinding halt.

For a while.

What happened next was the bloodiest urban massacre in Communist China's history. Unverifiable estimates range from hundreds to thousands of people killed at the hands, wheels, bludgeons, and bullets of the Chinese army. They are unverifiable thus far because the Chinese government claims the bloodletting never took place. It is a country where history is rewritten by proclamation, where news is managed in order to keep trading partnerships with other countries. But there are photos. Eyewitness accounts of those who escaped.

And there is a new interest in Christianity. According

to one news account, Protestant churches in the major cities of China were inundated with inquiries from students during the last six months of 1989. One teacher was quoted as saying, "In five years in China I have never seen anything like it. It was an explosion of interest in the Christian faith." Churches, the teacher said, "are just overwhelmed by the numbers coming to the services."

Other accounts told of entire dormitories converting to Christianity in many Chinese universities. Students who were demanding a change in Communism's domination of China were also looking for the meaning of life.

"In light of this full-blown skepticism in Communism, there is today a rare opportunity to penetrate the ideological walls that have kept China isolated from the gospel for centuries," said a 1990 report from Trans World Radio.

The Church of the Nazarene had been sponsoring a TWR program in China called Daily Inspiration for more than a year when the massacre took place. The program was five minutes long and gave brief answers to questions about the nature of God, atheism, and Christianity. During the time of the civil unrest, the programs focused on the peace that Jesus gives, the love of God, and how faith sees us through difficult times. The purpose was to cause people to think about their lives and to think about what they believed.

"As a result of listening to your gospel broadcasts for a long time and thinking a lot, I have found that we can enjoy life genuinely only if we take eternity as the goal in our lives," wrote one listener. "Daily Inspiration has helped me unravel some of my puzzles." Another wrote that the program was "better than proverbs and mottoes."

In 1991 the church expanded its reach into China by sponsoring a daily 30-minute TWR program called "The Good Earth." The sponsorship is shared by the Asia Pacific Nazarene Region, the Church of the Nazarene in Taiwan, and the World Mission Radio offering. The program is broadcast from the island of Guam with multiple signals so that it reaches the entire People's Republic. Letters have come in from every Chinese province and several surrounding countries. The name "The Good Earth" is derived from the knowledge that approximately 80 percent of the nation's 1.1 billion people are farmers. The program is targeted for the 18- to 40-year-old age-group, primarily people who have never lived outside of Communism. Since the gospel is a new concept to many listeners, the program is designed to lead listeners to a relationship with Christ. The speaker, Larry Hsieh, uses newspaper and magazine articles to discuss events and then presents what he calls a "three-month gospel cycle." For instance, each July university students take examinations; passing the examinations is perhaps the only means young people have for finding acceptable employment. Like other Asian cultures, high value is placed on employment and social status. To fail the exams is to bring disgrace upon the students and their families, and likely results in mind-numbing jobs in factories or farms. Some prefer suicide to life after a failed examination.

So in the spring, Hsieh discusses anxiety before exams and offers advice on how to prepare for them. The advice continues until May, and in June he discusses how to relax and answer exam questions. After exam time he talks more specifically about the gospel and poses the question, "What is success?" This opens the door for Hsieh to give his testimony and tell how eternal success is possible through Christ. In the aftermath of the Tiananmen Square incident, Hsieh drew a parallel with the gap between the Chinese people and the Chinese government to the gap between God and humanity. "How do we get back to God?" he asked in his program. Several programs then addressed how to enter into fellowship with the Heavenly Father.

"I heard the report of the Tiananmen Square incident through your program," wrote a listener from Myanmar (formerly Burma). "'The Good Earth' was my news media for that information. *Time* magazine wrote that Communism is exposed as a lie. I believe that our mighty God will have the last word." A Chinese man wrote, "We are sad about the events that transpired this year. All we can do is diligently preach the gospel. I hope that our descendants will be saved . . . We continue to gather, and the number of believers is growing. Most of them are helped by your gospel broadcasting."

Hsieh, who was born in mainland China, believes the biggest problem among Chinese young people is a refusal to believe in God. Other recurring questions asked by listeners are, if God is real, why are we suffering here? What good is God to me? Can He give me bread or education? Why is there factional fighting among the many Christian denominations? How do science and religion live together?

"I use every possible tool to remove these stones from their hearts," Hsieh was quoted as saying in one publication.

But sometimes, the stones come from something less weighty than atheism or creation. They can be similar to those experienced in churches around the world, whether belief in God is outlawed or encouraged. And it almost always has nothing really to do with God. A couple in their 60s wrote that they were having a difficult time knowing what direction their hands should be facing when they worship. "We have been taught to put our hands in a downward position when we worship the Lord," the lady wrote. "You have indicated that we could put our hands together—clasping them—as we worship the Lord . . . Our leader here says to raise your head toward Jesus with hands down in order to really praise Him. I am confused."

But other letters indicate that the *true* purpose of the broadcast is being received in the way it was intended. "As I have listened recently I have felt increasingly that I can no longer be merely an inactive listener," one man wrote. "I am at a point in my life when I must know something for sure about the reality of God for my life. I need your help because I am at this point truly adrift on the sea of life without the sure anchor of which you speak." Another wrote that when he first heard the program, "I felt I had been brought into a holy temple."

According to the volume of mail to the TWR office, "The Good Earth" is consistently the most popular TWR program broadcast to China. One listener told of how the program made him aware of his sin.

"At Easter time I opened my heart as I knelt down in front of my radio," he wrote. "Under your direction, as I wept, I accepted Christ as my personal Savior. I pray that the Lord will give me enduring faith and power to live. I'm asking God to open the hearts of my family so they will also repent and accept Him. May God help me find a church so I can be with the body of Christ where people encourage each other and praise the Lord together."

Other letters show how important the radio messages have become. "My sister has recently become a Christian," one man wrote. "My advice to her was that she get a radio immediately and start to listen to your programs regularly."

A woman from Myanmar wrote that there was great openness to the gospel in China. "Two of us believers went into China to share the gospel there," she wrote. "It was my first such trip. I found people really eager to hear. Three young people that we contacted at that time came into a personal relationship with the Lord."

"In a few months' time, some of us are hoping to spread the gospel to others," a young person from China wrote. "I hope you can send me some literature that deals with God as Creator. In our country we have no such literature."

Another woman wrote, "I live in one of the most remote villages in this province. Actually there are only about 20 families who live here, and we seldom see outsiders. So you can well imagine that evangelizing groups do not get this far. Although I had accepted the Lord long ago, I had become really cold for lack of spiritual nourishment. My church is poor and inactive. When I was at the end of myself I happened to tune in to your station and found there the uplift for my heart that I so needed."

A listener from Malaysia wrote, "My spiritual life is very dependent on my keeping in touch with your station."

A woman from China said, "I was always an idol worshiper in the past. But I praise the Lord that I had a chance to hear your programs. I listened to your presentation of the gospel and began to understand that idols had no way to help me. You taught me how to pray. I followed your instructions and gave my life to the Lord after I confessed my sins to Him. I then threw away the incense burner, the joss sticks, and the idol, taking Jesus to be my Savior."

How does God personally communicate through the programs?

"Two years ago I was listening to your program as usual when all of a sudden I felt a terrible storm raging in my heart," wrote one listener. "I knew that the death of Jesus on that Cross was for me and my sins. I dropped to my knees, weeping, and accepted the Lord into my heart. It was the greatest moment of my life."

The church's effort to reach the people of China goes back to days before the sponsorship of Trans World Radio programs, though. In the late 1970s Timothy and Pearl Yeh left China for the United States. With the help of Paul Skiles, the Yehs recorded gospel messages and music in Kansas City. Those programs were broadcast from various Asian studios to the mainland.

"Their being fresh out of the country, where they knew the needs and concerns of the people, made them a timely and providential resource for us," said Skiles. "They had an understanding for what things were like in China at the time, and they could give a spiritual message based on that understanding."

Timothy Yeh said that the broadcasts concentrated on salvation, love, freedom of the spirit, and creationism.

"In China they wanted to deny Jesus, Christianity, and God through study, even when they had no proof," Yeh said. "When I lived there we had no church, no preaching, and a law against listening to shortwave radio. This gave me a great concern for the lost souls of my country. Radio was a very good medium to reach them because radio can cover a large area more quickly than an individual preacher can." He said he tried to communicate what a relationship with Christ was like.

"Many people have never tasted truth and true love," he said. "In China they view man as a super animal. I wanted to show them that man is more than an animal—that he has a spirit and a soul."

When the Yehs moved to California, the sponsorship of the Trans World Radio programs began.

In other parts of Asia, radio is used as a ministry tool for pastors. In Indonesia, for example, where radio has been used consistently since 1980, programs are written, recorded, and broadcast by Nazarenes who use radio as a supplementary ministry avenue for their local churches. Soon those programs will be available on audiocassette and offered to radio stations in key cities.

But the dire need in Asia, as it is throughout the world in regard to radio ministry, is finding and training people to use radio effectively. The goal in Taiwan, for instance, is to train pastors to produce their own programs and beam them to the mainland.

"My dream would be to have a pastor preach a sermon on the radio, then send his sermon notes, or a list for further reading, to listeners so they could get into the Bible more directly," said George Rench, director for the Asia-Pacific Region. "But we need to be able to train people to do it."

At the Asia-Pacific Nazarene Theological Seminary, plans are being made for a media center that would have classrooms for courses in mass communications, studios for producing programs, and facilities for training pastors in how to use the media as part of their ministry when they return to their home countries.

"We have a building we can use and the funding to remodel it so it will be usable, but what we are waiting for is a person trained in communications who could make it work," said Rench.

In Korea a recording and training studio was opened in 1992 at the Nazarene Theological College there.

"We are in the process of reestablishing a national radio voice for the Church of the Nazarene," said Tim Mercer, who teaches at the college and oversees the new communications effort. Mercer was a ham radio operator as a youngster, so this new development plays right into his long-held interest. The national voice for the church would give the denomination a higher name recognition among Koreans, along with a broader platform for explaining holiness living. Eventually there could be two emphases in the programming: one would be as an evangelism tool directed at North Korea, and the other could be a discipleship tool for those who are believers, Mercer said.

Another benefit of the new center is in training students to write and record for radio, to speak in such a manner that is suitable for the medium, and to know what to do when radio networks come to them with offers of airtime for religious programs.

"We are going largely on the experience of what has worked in other parts of the world," said Mercer. "We'll be using students to help with follow-up of letters from listeners and with developing programs that will uniquely appeal to Asian audiences."

In Papua New Guinea, a communications center was recently built at the Nazarene Bible College there. The use of radio as a ministry tool was immediately put into part of the curriculum for the students.

"This is a training school for pastors, so it was natural to include radio as part of the training," said Gordon Johnston, the area's mission director. Students are taught how to put together a radio broadcast and are trained in how to speak clearly over the airwaves.

"There is an opportunity through the radio stations in this country right now, so we needed to respond quickly," Johnston said. "It is the perfect time in this country's history for us to be increasing our involvement with radio."

The goals for the communications training are to help pastors become comfortable in a radio studio and to develop the ministry into a broader programming effort where tapes of broadcasts can be offered to radio stations around the country.

"Ninety-five percent of communication in this country is through radio," Johnston said. "The time is right for us to be training people now."

6

New Beginnings for Ancient Lands

JORDAN

The Persian Gulf War of 1991 left images permanently etched in the memories of people around the world. Reporters donning gas masks, baby cribs draped in clear plastic, missiles colliding over cities and military bases, thousands of soldiers stopping their military duties to bow to Mecca for midday prayers, live reports of air raids over Baghdad, and black smoke from oil fires blocking out the sunlight in Kuwait City all painted a horrifying picture of what modern war was like.

The war left one other impression as well. "Masterdesign," the low-key conversational radio program produced in Indiana in the U.S. (see chapter 2), was broadcast from Cyprus to the troops in Saudi Arabia. The response to the program throughout the Middle East was so positive that the Church of the Nazarene believed it was a sign that the area was ripe for regular broadcasts proclaiming Christ to the predominantly Muslim countries.

Jacob Ammari, then district superintendent for the region, was appointed director of the new radio effort and spent several weeks in intensive training at the Trans World Radio studios in Monte Carlo. In March 1992 the first locally produced Nazarene radio program was broadcast from Cyprus to the Middle East. Within a week letters came from listeners in Egypt, Iraq, Syria, Turkey, Sudan, Saudi Arabia, Israel, and Jordan.

Ammari, whose base is in Amman, Jordan, said that in the first six weeks of the broadcasts, he sent out 600 books to listeners who wrote for more information on becoming a Christian. He keeps an active correspondence with those who write, and he retains their addresses for future contact regarding starting a new church.

"Ninety percent of the letters contained at least this sentence: 'This is great—we need it,'" Ammari said. "Many asked how they could be saved."

Knowing that most of the listeners would be of the Muslim faith, Ammari said that he had to start from a common level of understanding.

"Muslims believe in God, but not in the Trinity," he said. "They believe in Jesus as a prophet. They do not understand redemption through the cross of Jesus. So to speak to them, you have to have some kind of base.

"In their Koran there are many stories of the Old Testament, so I started the broadcasts with the Book of Genesis." He tied the Old Testament stories to New Testament truths in Christ.

"In Genesis 1, where God makes man in His image, Muslims get confused because they ask, 'How can God create in His image when He has no image? How can a picture of God exist?' I speak their language and put it in terms they can relate to."

A listener from Cairo concurred. "I listened to your program, which was discussing the Book of Genesis, and felt rest in my heart and enjoyment in hearing," she wrote. "We do need such explanations."

A man from Iraq wrote, "I was so pleased of hearing those blessed thoughts of your program. What really differs your effective program is simplicity and clearness to reach the hearts of listeners with the word of the Holy Bible."

Another Iraqi listener was more blunt in his appreciation: "You extricated me from the filthy mud through your program. I truly thank you."

Ammari likens his task of broadcasting to the Arabic-speaking world to God's people when they encountered Jericho on their way to Canaan.

"Joshua and his people were worried, frightened, and questioning among themselves," he said. "'How can we jump over these high walls or break them down to win the city to the Lord? We have not had much experience for such an assignment, and the tools we have are not available.' A few weeks later the whole nation was excited to see the destruction of the walls of that rebellious city of Jericho in a miraculous way."

Then, in recent years when the Berlin Wall came down, and the Eastern European Iron Curtain was removed, Ammari noted that some walls remained.

"There are nondemocratic countries where you cannot cross their borders with your Arabic Bible," he said. "You cannot even hold an Arabic Bible study in some countries—not even in your own home. Distribution of Christian tracts is forbidden, and the effort to convert or even talk about Christ and share your experience with Him is not allowed."

Using radio as a means for telling the Good News is one of the ways to get over those walls.

"Radio broadcasts jump over all thorny fences carrying the message of the love of Christ to the hearts and lives of people without even needing to knock on doors," he said. "It is the most active tool to ruin all created hindering walls. We have seen the walls of Communism torn down—I want to see the remaining stumbling blocks removed as well."

Some areas have such fanatic groups influencing the government that they will imprison those who choose a faith other than Muslim.

"These are some of the walls I want to see removed," Ammari said. This is an important region to reach for

Christ because of the hostility toward the gospel at one level and the hunger for it at another level. And, historically, it has been a place where God has seen His people through difficult times.

It is where Jacob wrestled with an angel. It is where Saul met his match on the road to Damascus. It is where Moses stood, high above the Promised Land, on Mount Nebo. It is where Ruth and Boaz met. It is where God has been intervening for thousands of years. He intervened through times of testing, times of difficulty, times of certain failure, times of perseverance and faith.

"I can envision a spiritual revolution in the souls of millions," Ammari said. "The vision is becoming more clear."

ENGLAND

In his home country of England, John Wesley would travel from town to town on a horse, telling people that they could have a personal relationship with Jesus Christ. Over the years, thousands were reached by his traveling and his holding special services to accommodate the crowds. Now, in that same country, a new development could provide the gospel message every day to millions of listeners.

A recent law passed by the British Parliament allows, for the first time, religious broadcasters to own radio stations, sponsor programs, and buy advertising time. Rev. Frederick Grossmith, a Nazarene pastor in Cleethorpes, lobbied the ruling body and helped influence the decision. He argued his case before the Court of Human Rights and even appeared on national television to present his views.

"It is a new era of unparalleled opportunity for Christian broadcasting in Britain," he said. "Radio has gotten a new lease on life."

In the next few years the British government will license 300 new independent and community radio stations.

As a result of the government's new openness, a Nazarene Radio Advisory Board was organized. It includes district superintendents from the north and south regions, and Grossmith as the chairman.

Grossmith's involvement in Christian broadcasting goes back a few years. In 1986 he was elected general secretary of the Christian Broadcasting Council of the United Kingdom. It is a group of Christians involved in the media who desire to see the gospel broadcast through the nation, and Christian members of the government have aligned themselves with the group.

"Through them we have a voice in the nation," he said.

He became interested in using radio as a ministry tool when he was interviewed on several radio programs because of the popularity of books he had written. When people responded to him on the street, he saw how influential the medium could be.

"The interviews became talking points for people," he said. "When the gas meter man told me he heard me on the radio, I knew there was something to this."

He began broadcasting his own programs and recalled an incident that further proved his point.

"I had a man in my church who came with his believing wife but didn't like my preaching," Grossmith said. "It hit the target. He wouldn't admit at the time that it scratched where he itched. Nevertheless, he persevered by coming, if not under protest, each Sunday. One day he told me, smiling, that he would be away for some months as his company had asked him to work in Cyprus. One day after work he switched his radio on, tuned to the British Broadcasting Corporation (BBC) Overseas Service, and homed in on one of my broadcasts. Later he told me that he threw his arms up in the air and shouted, 'I can't get away from that man' and accepted Jesus as his Savior!"

The BBC asked Grossmith to participate in a 30-minute program on "Ghosts, Demons, and Things That Go

Bump in the Night" before a live studio audience of teenagers. The format of the program allowed Grossmith to tell of the dangers of the occult, and particularly of Yoga, which he said can lead to occultism and spiritism.

"The presenter thought I was joking," he said. "All else was forgotten and that became the program. About three weeks later a producer telephoned me to see if I would be willing to take part in a program dealing with life after death. Before getting off the line she told me that, as a result of the previous program, numerous complaints were made to the station by Yoga clubs. Some smaller ones were on the point of closing, and the larger ones were moaning about a marked drop in attendance."

What is needed to capitalize on the new freedoms afforded religious broadcasting in England are qualified people to write, produce, and broadcast programs. Training people in the use of mass media is taking place at the European Nazarene Bible College, and the goal is to offer mass communication courses as part of the college's curriculum. The training includes how to follow up on listeners who write to the program and how to get listeners plugged into local churches.

"The most common misuse of the radio medium by Christians, especially preachers, is to treat the listening audience as an extension to Sunday's congregation," said Grossmith. "When preachers see a microphone, they think they are Billy Graham!"

What is necessary is training communicators to write and speak as if there were one listener.

"Jesus was an expert communicator," he said. "He knew the value of a premise, the core of your message. We see it in every parable He told. Each time we see a TV commercial or hear a good story, there is a premise. A premise consists of a subject, an active verb, and an object. For example, 'Love conquers hate.'

"Because the atmosphere of a studio, the sight of a microphone, and the experience of wearing headphones can put them off, communications training is a requirement!"

The key to success in England is identifying qualified people to be involved and in convincing Christians there that the medium is worth supporting.

"We have had this bondage of prohibition regarding religious broadcasting for so long that we are like the children of Israel who became used to being slaves in Egypt," Grossmith said. "Radio has never been more popular or more available. Now is the time to build upon our new-found freedoms."

7

Message Received

AFRICA

There's irony in the Bill Wagner story. Before he accepted Christ he worked in electronics for the University of Wyoming and had a small television and radio repair business. While he worked in his shop, he would spin through the dial of his shortwave radio until he found something he liked. One night he found a program called "Unshackled," which re-created stories about people's sinful lives and their conversions. The program was broadcast from one of the world's religious superstations, HCJB in Quito, Ecuador, on the other side of the equator.

"I had grown tired of the local stations, and this one caught my attention," he said.

Before too many years passed, he was in South Africa as a missionary for the Church of the Nazarene producing radio programs, trying to see if there were more Bill Wagners out there with their radios on.

"When I got saved it seemed that everyone around me had a place of ministry where they could fit in," he said. "I kept asking, 'What can I do? Where do I fit in?' That's a dangerous thing to ask the Lord," he said, laughing. "The Lord can use anybody who is willing."

Wagner was part of the beginning of the increased emphasis on radio in Africa. Before his arrival in the mid-

1970s, radio efforts were handled by pastors and missionaries, and there was not much enthusiasm for the task.

"No one really had the time or training to work effectively in radio, because everyone had their full-time jobs," Wagner said. Then he added with a laugh, "The person elected as coordinator was usually whichever missionary was on furlough!"

When Wagner arrived as a missionary, given the task of building a radio ministry, he had a couple of cassette recorders and traveled around to cities and villages so pastors could put messages on tape.

"I realized how different things were from the university system when I had to use a fork in a tree limb to hold the microphone," Wagner said. Once the messages were recorded he would take the tapes to a Trans World Radio studio for production. Before long, he had built a studio in Johannesburg and was traveling with homemade sound barriers tied to the top of his car so he could get better quality recordings on location.

The response to the programs was encouraging. A farmer who had been listening to the programs wrote that he had been looking for ways to tell his workers about Jesus, and wondered if he could get cassettes of the programs to play at mealtime. Sherrill Wagner, who is married to Bill, and handled the correspondence, sent copies of the programs and the farmer played the tapes for his workers. People from other farms heard about the programs and came to listen as well. Soon the farmer had more than 100 people coming just to hear the tapes.

"Radio is to Africa what television is to the U.S.," Wagner said. "It connects people to the outside world."

Wagner returned to the U.S. in the late 1980s, and Harald Biesenbach of Germany was appointed director of Nazarene Communications Services in Africa. Biesenbach had been a student at European Nazarene Bible College and became interested in full-time ministry. Like Wagner, Biesenbach didn't know specifically what that meant.

"Essentially, I wanted to work for the Lord," he said. "So I kept looking for places where I could be used. I never felt a call to go into missions; the Lord didn't come to the edge of my bed and say, 'Harald, I want you to be a missionary in Africa.' I had a desire in my heart, which I believe came from the Lord." He now coordinates programming and training in South Africa, Zimbabwe, Malawi, Kenya, and the Cape Verde Islands. Plans are underway to expand communication service to east and west Africa as well.

In Johannesburg the communications office produces 11 weekly 15-minute programs in seven languages. "The Happy Side," one of the original programs, is an upbeat, encouraging friend to thousands of listeners.

"I love your program on the radio," one listener wrote. "I know there is a message, a word of encouragement, a laugh, or something to share with someone during the day." Other programs include Bible studies, modern music, dramatizations, as well as traditional programs that have sermons and hymns.

"Thank you very much for feeding us spiritually after we have done daily duties," a listener wrote. "It is like teaching us to thank God before we go to sleep."

Another was moved by the encouragement received over the air.

"Brother, your words are encouraging to us as Christians to stand firm for Jesus, no matter what we face. It is my prayer that the Lord continue to be with you and your programs, as you plan every day."

And while the programs don't overtly address the political and racial tensions that exist in the continent, Biesenbach sees a parallel between the broadcasts and the prophets of the Old Testament.

"The prophets spoke against the corruption of their day, and we see the same kind of corruption today in the oppression that exists," he said. "We don't do political programs, but if you preach a gospel that addresses interpersonal behavior, you get your point across. Jesus was for all people."

The point got across to this listener, "I do not let even one program skip me. Thank you very much for your messages, songs, and prayers that took me out of the slavery of sin. I love your music programs and your sermons."

Another wrote, "I would like to encourage you to carry on with your wonderful service because it really changes the listeners' way of behavior, and I am one of such people."

Some of the listeners ask for cassettes of specific programs, some ask for advice, some ask for Bible study materials. All letters are answered and then passed along to pastors in the area who, when possible, can arrange a personal visit. "We are a tool for every local congregation in their church growth enterprises," Biesenbach said.

The programs are also targeting areas where there is not yet a Nazarene work but where one is planned. Biesenbach has seen firsthand how effective it is to have radio open the door to the gospel.

"Radio speaker Rev. Benjamin Ngqakayi came with me to Khayalitsha, a township of 400,000 people just outside of a metropolitan area," Biesenbach recalled in a letter. "We were going from house to house witnessing and inviting people in the community to services that evening. In house after house there was a tremendous response as the people recognized Rev. Ngqakayi from his radio programs in the Xhosa language. Radio had prepared the way for the planting of a church.

"There were 88 in our first service. One year later we had a church building and 60 people are worshiping each week in this new church, pastored by a recent Bible college graduate. Radio indeed paved the way for this church planting endeavor."

In Liberia, where civil war destroyed most communication facilities, radio stations are again looking for program suppliers. Recordings were made recently to put Nazarene programs on the air in that war-ravaged country. Likewise, as Angola is more open to Christian messages after Communist rule, radio is being used as a way to prepare for the new work being planned by the Church of the Nazarene for that country.

In Zimbabwe, where radio messages are heard throughout the country over the government-run airwaves, Mark Taylor, a Nazarene pastor, is chairman of the nation's religious advisory board.

"The opportunities are there to have an impact on the whole nation," he said. "The state-run radio is *very* open to religious programming because the government sees Christianity as a way to propel morality in the country."

The openness is welcome, because in the mid-1980s a denomination pressured the Zimbabwe government into giving them enormous media coverage for a large crusade in return for a medical team to come to perform open-heart surgeries.

"They got the airtime, the heart team came, and the two-week-long rally was held, but five years later people at the broadcasting center still talked disparagingly about the [denomination]," Taylor said.

Taylor records and produces his own programs, and is involved in a live religious talk show. The show addresses specific issues faced in life as a Christian, and most of the themes revolve around what Christians believe.

"The response to that program has been overwhelming," he said.

After one program, a listener called Taylor and told him she was about to commit suicide, but the message she heard made her reconsider.

"I was pretty new to the pastorate at the time and didn't know what to do," he said. "So I just prayed for her over the telephone." Four years later she asked if Taylor would officiate at her wedding.

"I don't need any convincing of the power of radio," he said.

One listener wrote that the programs made him and several others want to become Nazarenes.

"I am a member of a certain church branch in Zimbabwe in Matebeland South Province with 200 followers (Christians). We are very interested in listening to the radio ministry of the Church of the Nazarene, that we even want to join you friends. Keep up your standards. I want to have an interview with the director of the radio ministry of the Church of the Nazarene concerning the problems that are facing us, for example, that we do not have a Church of the Nazarene, as we wish to join you totally."

Taylor has also been involved in arranging for an international version of "Focus on the Family" and "Masterdesign," both of which take a discussion format.

"In the old days it was good enough to put a 45-minute sermon on the air and people would listen to it," Taylor said. "That doesn't work anymore. What is needed now are dramas, music, even ways to use radio for extension teaching." Biesenbach and Taylor agree that the most crucial need today in radio work is for more people who can write and produce programs.

A phrase that Biesenbach likes to recite in relation to training is, "Give a hungry person a fish and you have satisfied his need once. Teach him how to fish and he will benefit forever." Put another way, "There is a need and a place for full-time ministry in broadcasting," Taylor said.

One of the most popular programs, "Search the Scriptures," a weekly Bible study, was taken off the air recently when the person who wrote and recorded the program returned to his home country. It was a program that generated up to 2,000 letters per month. Another program, designed for children, needed scripts so a missionary got a group of students at Trevecca Nazarene College to write them.

"We desperately need committed and qualified personnel," said Biesenbach.

Part of the answer can be in training pastors in mass communication techniques. The Far Eastern Broadcasting Corporation provides courses in writing and speaking, and four pastors from Zimbabwe recently received training.

Biesenbach hopes that communication training can become part of the curriculum at Nazarene regional Bible colleges.

"We need to build our pool of people who can work in radio," Taylor said. "We need to take advantage of the enormous freedoms that are there for us. We must move from canned, imported programs to locally produced programs with local voices and accents."

Throughout the continent pastors are being invited by governments and private stations to participate in radio and television efforts.

"If the people we send aren't acceptable because of lack of training, they won't get invited back," said Biesenbach. "We can't afford to blow our chance."

The present opportunity calls for hearts to be open to the leading of God. It calls for a realization similar to the one Bill Wagner had during a particularly difficult time in the early days of African Nazarene Radio. He had arranged to drive into an extremely remote area so that the pastors there could record their messages. The plan was for Wagner to then take those recordings back to his studio, put music with them, and send them to stations that could broadcast into even more remote areas where that language and dialect was spoken.

"I drove for a couple of very hard days, and when I got there, no one was ready," Wagner said. "I waited around for a week, and no one even showed up." Disgusted, frustrated, and angry, Wagner drove to the nearby Kruger National Park and told God what he thought.

"I said to God, 'I quit. I'm through. I'm going home.'" But God had a reply.

"He said, 'How do you think *I* feel? *I* was counting on *you!*'" Message received, Wagner thought. And he stayed.

INDIA

Malcolm Muggeridge, an influential Christian thinker and writer from England, said in 1925 that it was impossible to go to India and avoid thinking. For centuries people from around the world have gone to that country on spiritual and intellectual quests, searching for answers to eternal questions. Muggeridge did. Thomas Merton did. So have countless other evangelical thinkers, teachers, and writers.

Mahatma Gandhi of India remains one of the world's most revered and thoughtful spiritual and political leaders. His teachings, which borrowed from Hindu, Buddhism, and Christianity, proposed that change could occur when each person becomes transformed into a new man or woman by the teachings of peace and nonviolence. Millions have adopted those teachings.

Mother Teresa, a Catholic nun who spends most of her time with the sick and dying of Calcutta, attracts thousands of visitors to the areas where she helps. Organizations patterned after her work in Calcutta have opened in the poor sections of Tijuana, Detroit, and other centers of poverty around the world. As Gandhi was before her, she is viewed as one to whom seekers and thinkers alike are drawn.

Despite the dominance of the Hindu, Muslim, and Catholic faiths in that country, second in population only to China, there has been great openness to radio broadcasts written and produced by the Church of the Nazarene. The most established program has been broadcast for more than 40 years, "Tilak and Christ." Tilak is the name of a well-known poet who converted to Christianity. Though his conversion caused him to be an instant minority, Tilak's poems and songs remained popular.

In 1952 a program based on his work was put on the air by the Church of the Nazarene, and, though it told how the poet found Christ, it found a sizable audience among Hindus. When the program was made into a weekly, more than 500 responses came in from listeners.

Rev. M. V. Ingle has coordinated the radio effort practically from its beginning, and he responds to those who write by giving encouragement, telling where local churches can be found, and providing materials for doing Bible studies at home. More than 3,000 people have done the study course. He also travels to visit groups of listeners and gives seminars on the Bible and following Christ.

"I have completed the Bible correspondence course and received a most valuable book (a Bible) from you, which I read regularly," wrote a Hindu man. "On the first page of the Bible you have sent you have written 'Repent and be baptized in the name of Jesus, so that your sins may be forgiven.' Now I have an opportunity to be baptized and be His sheep. I praise God."

A Catholic priest was so moved by the program that he asked for a transcript of the message on "Sin, Condemnation, and Forgiveness." He also asked for cassettes of music and other messages. "Please send me some material, useful for the spiritual harvest," he wrote.

This person's letter had fruitful results, "Ours is the only Christian family in our village without a pastor and church nearby," the listener wrote. "Our radio serves as our pastor and the radio program as our worship time. We are listening to your series of messages, 'What It Means to Be a Christian.' It became clear to me that we are only Christian by name but that it must become a reality. We are looking forward to your guidance." Ingle and others visited this family and others like it, resulting in a "Nazarene Radio Worship Fellowship." Through this two churches were formed in 1991, and a new district was formed in the area in early 1992.

Other programs by India Nazarene Radio include a locally produced "Showers of Blessing" and "Ladder to Heaven."

Ingle states that radio is an effective means for spreading the gospel for at least these six reasons:

1. Radio has an unlimited dimension. It is not limited by geographic areas. It need not fit into a political mold. It can penetrate and captivate people's minds in unexpected and otherwise inaccessible places.
2. It does not matter whether the individual is in an

urban environment or in the back woods. He may be rich or a beggar, educated or illiterate. He may be on the battlefield or enjoying the luxury of his normal life. He may be behind the curtain or enjoying full religious freedom. The long arms of radio can put the gospel into his hands, no matter what his situation is.

3. Radio has power to reach the individual who has never heard of Christ, or who has no desire or interest to hear. The same is true in reaching the recluse, the fearful, and even the one who hates the gospel.

4. Each radio center can present Christ as Savior in a new way, from different standpoints and in a multiplicity of methods. Radio can reach hearts, minds, and cultures. It can reveal individual needs. Weak hope can be fanned into life-giving certainty because of this medium.

5. The radio message can simultaneously reach people located in many places who have different thought patterns and attitudes. Many can, and do, become acquainted with Christ in this way, for not only the written Word but the spoken Word can prepare individual minds for concrete decisions.

6. Radio is a natural means by which the purity of our doctrine can be imparted both to those who are newly converted and to those who are actually only Christian in name. Thus a foundation can be established and constant growth in faith and Christian life nourished. We are committed to winning souls for Christ and nourishing their spiritual lives. Radio is a custom-made tool to achieve this goal.

What Ingle observes about the reach of radio to diverse groups is borne out in letters he has received recently.

"I experience myself in a totally different atmosphere while listening to your program," one person wrote. "I want to make friends with you. Can you make friendship with me? I am beginning to like Christ."

A Hindu man testified to the power of prayer in his Hindu home. "I listened to your program regularly and was attracted toward Christ. But my orthodox wife did not want to give up our Hindu faith. I did not know how to change her mind. But as you said in one of the programs, I kept on singing the songs which come on your program and prayed. God heard yours and my prayer. My wife changed her mind. Myself, my wife, and our two children believed in Jesus. We took baptism. We have 15 more persons in our family. They haven't yet believed in Jesus, but every night they sit together with us and sing the songs of Jesus. We trust that one day they will also believe in Jesus."

A soldier guarding one of India's borders requested copies of songs and messages to help him grow in his faith. "Life is always unsure, but I listen to your program regularly and feel satisfied," he wrote.

A Muslim girl, knowing the personal price a person can pay for considering other faiths, took the risk of corresponding with Ingle so her friends wouldn't get into trouble. Then she added her own personal request.

"My friend and a younger sister want to do the Bible correspondence courses," she wrote. "They wish to know more about Christ but are not able to correspond with you because of opposition in the family. So please send their lesson to my address. Please pray for them and me."

The radio programs have been instrumental in changing people's lives. Ingle told of one man, a schoolteacher, who was so burdened with his personal and family problems that he thought the only solution was to leave his home and family. After hearing "Tilak and Christ" one morning, though, he showed up at Ingle's office unexpectedly. Ingle talked with him and gave him the first lesson in the Bible study course.

"He has found happiness and decided to stay with the family," Ingle said.

Another man, who hadn't intended to listen to the program, heard it only because he was an electrician and his job that day had him working at a restaurant. "Tilak and Christ" was playing over the restaurant's sound system. Now he's attending a Bible study.

Sometimes the program is played in jail. A government worker who, while drunk, had burned his wife to death, heard "Tilak and Christ" while he was waiting for his trial. He wrote for the Bible correspondence course and read through the Bible three times. He found Christ and, through a series of miracles, was freed from jail. Soon after he gave his testimony in the Wanowrie Church of the Nazarene in Poona.

So while India remains a country that attracts thinking and spiritually hungry people, many are finding that, like Muggeridge did, one must choose between a religion like Hinduism, with its logical explanations, and Christianity, with its unexplainable love from God through Christ. Thousands, like Muggeridge and Tilak, are choosing Christ.

8

For the One Who
Waits and Listens

The power of a radio message was impressed on Ray Hendrix early in his life. He was four, living in Buenos Aires, Argentina, with his missionary parents, Spurgeon and Faye Hendrix. It was December 7, 1941, and his terrified family had been listening to radio news about the bombing of Pearl Harbor in Hawaii. He remembers seeing his father move the dial of the shortwave radio up a few frequencies and stop at HCJB, the powerful station in Quito, Ecuador, just in time to hear a man and woman singing in English:

> *Be not dismayed whate'er betide;*
> *God will take care of you.*
> *Beneath His wings of love abide;*
> *God will take care of you.*
>
> *God will take care of you,*
> *Thro' ev'ryday, O'er all the way.*
> *He will take care of you;*
> *God will take care of you.*

No matter what may be the test,
God will take care of you.
Lean, weary one, upon His breast;
God will take care of you.

God will take care of you,
Thro' ev'ryday, O'er all the way.
He will take care of you;
God will take care of you.

As other examples throughout this book have shown, it was the right message at the right time. A few decades later, Hendrix became the director of the Nazarene radio effort. It is an effort that now proclaims the Good News to the following languages and dialects:

Spanish—20 program formats
English—7 program formats
Portuguese—3 program formats
French
Creole
Italian
Greek
Arabic
Armenian
Chinese (Mandarin)
Russian
Quechua
Aymara
Shuar
K'ekchi
Pokomchi
Ilocano
Waray
Cebuano
Ilongo
Tagalog
Bicolano

Visayan
Indonesian
Marathi
Tamil
Hindi
Bengali
Xhosa
Swahili
Zulu
Shangaans
Pedi
Tswana
Tsonga
Chechewa
Sesotho
Navajo
Thai

For the Church of the Nazarene to maintain these broadcasts and expand into other languages and formats, something needs to happen very soon. More people need to be trained in methods of using radio and other media as ministry tools. Training facilities need to be built, and teachers to train pastors need to come forward. People need to be trained in communicating to others who share the same language and culture.

This need was made clear to Hendrix during a trip in which he encountered a traveler from India, who lumped all evangelical broadcasting together in his assessment.

"The mistake you Christians made was not your message, because it's a good one, but it was your methods," the traveler told Hendrix. "First, you knew little, if anything about our religion of peace, meditation, love, and nonviolence. Second, you came in singing some very strange, frightening, and clashing songs, such as 'Onward Christian Soldiers, Marching as to War,' and an entire repertoire of songs dealing with blood shed from a cross, and how this blood cleanses from wrong. Then, third, you got around to explaining to us that it was really love that made a man you call 'Jesus Christ' die on our behalf to forgive us for all our sins. You should have started with that, and thought about the clashing songs and studied considerably more than you did about our religious roots."

What this shows is that the message of love and forgiveness crosses cultural barriers, but the method in which the message is proclaimed may not.

"Sometimes methodology can do more damage than good if proper awareness of a target culture has not first taken place," Hendrix said.

People from the countries where the message is being proclaimed need to be trained as writers, broadcasters, technicians, and producers so that the message can be relevant and sensitive to their culture. There are plans to increase the training through the Bible colleges around the world, but then there is the matter of cost to build and equip those facilities.

"We know that radio is a valuable tool," said George Rench, Asia-Pacific regional director. "But our biggest need in utilizing it is having enough people out there with a vision."

This book shows some of those people—Bill Wagner, Juan Vazquez-Pla, H. T. Reza, M. V. Ingle, T. W. Willingham, Ray Hendrix, Jorge Barros, and others who had the vision. It also shows some of those who are stepping into that vision—Giovanni Monterroso, Harald Biesenbach, Nikolaj Sawatzky, Phil Stout, Jerry Brewton, Mark Taylor, Frederick Grossmith, Jacob Ammari, and others.

Mrs. Louise Chapman, former missionary to Africa and former president of the Women's Foreign Missionary Society (now known as the NWMS), has a vision of her own.

"I know enough about talking with God to know when He is speaking to me," she said in 1992, just before her 100th birthday. "And He gave me this burden about reaching the lost through radio." She was affected by seeing countries that had historically shut out religious broadcasting show signs of openness to the gospel for the first time in decades. "God has moved ahead of us in ways we never imagined or dreamed possible," she said. "He has felled the immovable wall, rolled away the iron curtain, put the enemy to flight, and opened wide doors that have been, for years, securely bolted."

So why wasn't the church moving more quickly to capitalize on the new openness, she wondered?

"Here we have this wonderful gadget that God gave us, and we weren't using it to its potential," she said. Lack of people and lack of money to build the facilities to train them were the reasons. None of the Nazarene programs solicit funds over the air. They are paid for by World Mission Radio offerings, districts, and local churches.

It was such a substantial burden that, at the age of 96, she felt she needed to get away from her familiar surroundings at Casa Robles in California so she could be alone with God. She went to a friend's house in the desert to try to sort out what God was telling her.

"Sometimes if I pray and think and try to understand, the understanding comes all at once," she said. "And that's what happened." During her prayer time, God told her what He wanted.

"I have the absolute assurance that this is what God said to me," she affirmed. "He said, 'How would you like to give me $1 million for radio?' I said I thought it was something the church could do, but why me?" With that, she was reminded of Moses' confrontation with God in Exodus 3.

"God said, 'I've heard my people groaning. Come now. I'm sending you. And I'll go with you.'" She remembered hearing a sermon about the mantle before Elisha. "Elisha had to see the mantle and take possession of it," she recalls the preacher saying. And in her own paraphrase, she said, "We need to grab this opportunity by the beard—I'm afraid too often we wait and try for a tail hold."

With that, God gave Mrs. Chapman a number of ideas on how to raise the money, she said. One way was to get 40,000 Nazarenes to give $25.00 per year in addition to their annual World Mission Radio offering.

"Even poor people spend $25.00 on dinner," she said. "There are a million Nazarenes around the world, so finding 40,000 shouldn't be too difficult. Oh, how I long for us to move out of the 'progress as usual' and move into the land of great and unusual conquests for our Lord!"

She also is asking individuals and business people to give $100 or $1,000 to help commemorate her 100 years. One group she is particularly interested in is other senior citizens.

"There are thousands and thousands of seniors, and they aren't given much to do in their churches," she said. She proposes that seniors take on radio as a prayer and giving project. At least half of the 40,000 donors should be seniors, she said. "It would do them good," she said. "If they'd pray, God would give them more to do."

In addition, children should be involved in the $1 million project. "Children can be very effective in giving and praying," she said. "Getting children involved is a tremendous avenue for stirring up the local church." She sees potential for matching seniors with children in local churches to be prayer and giving partners for radio. Children need to have something to do in the life of the church too.

The million-dollar-per-year campaign will go toward establishing or improving communications centers that will have studios and classrooms for training local pastors and broadcast workers. They will be named the Louise Chapman Communication Centers.

"It bothers me to hear people say that, now that they have reached a certain age, they have done their part," she said. "Has *anyone* done his or her part who still has breath?"

I personally witnessed the power of proclaiming the gospel over the airwaves when I visited the homes of Elario Zugina (Introduction), Henri and Jeanna Torres (chapter 3) and Jorge and Cecelia Solis (chapter 4)—all radio listeners in Costa Rica who came to know Christ as a result of listening and responding.

The scene at the Solis's one-room metal shed of a house is etched permanently in my memory. After my interview with them we sat around the table and prayed, thanking God for the miracle of new life in Him, which we all had now experienced. I prayed in English. They prayed in Spanish. The songbirds in their cages created a deafening background of music. And though we did not understand what the other was saying on one level, the Solises, the birds, and I knew *exactly* what the other was saying! We wept in joy together because God was in that room, and language barriers couldn't keep us from celebrating that presence.

"Your journey is not to places—though intriguing and unique they are—it is to people," Paul Skiles wrote about Nazarene radio broadcasts. "And you have moved gently among them. Knowing intimately their mind and background and need. Speaking softly their language. Comforting, teaching, giving truth, encouragement, and hope. Showing the way. You are well-received even by those who had no advance notice and find you quite by accident. Some have learned the schedule of your arrivals and carefully arranged to be there. The exact number can never be known, and in some ways is beside the point, for how could you decide to disappoint even one who waits and listens alone in the darkness?"

Radio as a technology has been around for about 100 years. With expanding technology and popularity it has since become available to virtually every person on the planet. Hard as it may be to believe, in this society tied together by the mass media, there are still those who haven't heard the Good News. It may be awhile before someone tells them in person. Through radio, someone could tell them right now, while you read this.

As we did in the home of Jorge and Cecelia Solis, let us give thanks for what God has done through these radio broadcasts. But let's not stop with praise. There's a whole world to cover.

NOTES

1. Brother Andrew, *God's Smuggler* (The New American Library, Inc., for Nazarene Publishing House, Kansas City, 1967), 186.

2. Ibid., 180.